"A creative and insightful appro[...] how our food choices affect bot[...] economies. We hope that people will be inspired to take action locally, as this books shows that we all have a choice and that if we work together we have the capacity to tackle the major problems of hunger, waste and inequality."

Michelle Slater, Missio

"As more and more people are wondering how to live sustainably, this book couldn't come at a more relevant time. Claud Fullwood mixes together recipes, interviews, facts and personal experience into a delicious treat of a book: one which is light but substantial, and good for you too! By looking back to our grandparents' experience, she provides us with hope for the future and plenty of ideas about how to eat better, live more fully, and reconnect with the world around us and the people we love."

Sarah Hagger-Holt, author, parent-of-two and former campaigns manager at Catholic aid agency CAFOD

For my husband and children who make every
day something to celebrate
and
In loving memory of Jim

The
Rations
Challenge

Forty Days of Feasting in a Wartime Kitchen

Claud Fullwood

LION

Published by

Lion Hudson Limited

Wilkinson House, Jordan Hill Business Park

Banbury Road, Oxford OX2 8DR, England

www.lionhudson.com

ISBN 978 0 7459 8077 5

e-ISBN 978 0 7459 8082 9

First edition 2019

Acknowledgments

Scripture quotations [marked NIV] taken from the Holy Bible, New International Version Anglicized. Copyright © 1979, 1984, 2011 Biblica, formerly International Bible Society. Used by permission of Hodder & Stoughton Ltd, an Hachette UK company. All rights reserved. "NIV" is a registered trademark of Biblica. UK trademark number 1448790.

p.19 Quotation from Steve Goodier: http://www.LifeSupportSystem.com

p.42 "Why Shouldn't She" © Grace Nichols. Reproduced with permission from Curtis Brown Group Ltd on behalf of Grace Nichols (ebook rights)

"Why Shouldn't She" © Grace Nichols from *The Fat Black Woman's Poems* published by Virago; Little, Brown Group. (print rights)

p.66 Julia Child interview by Polly Frost, *Interview Magazine*, 16 July 2009.

Every effort has been made to trace copyright holders and to obtain their permission for the use of copyright material. The publisher apologizes for any errors or omissions in the above list and would be grateful if notified of any corrections that should be incorporated in future reprints or editions of this book.

A catalogue record for this book is available from the British Library
Printed and bound in the UK, October 2019, LH26

The Rations Challenge is not intended to be a diet book or meal plan. Please consult your doctor if you intend to make any changes to your diet.

Contents

Introduction

A few years ago, I found myself wondering how I could explore abstinence as an act of solidarity. What if abstinence could help me to change my perspective on how we live, how we shop, and how we eat?

So, for Lent that year, I decided to live on rations: 1943 British rations to be precise. Why? Well, apart from my being obsessed with all things vintage, the Second World War was most likely the last time there were real food shortages in this country, when the threat of hunger was a real issue for the whole of Britain. Although it was nothing like a starvation diet, by 1943, most food was rationed in the UK and almost no imports were getting in. I decided to live on rations for Lent and I wrote a blog about my experiences – some of which you can read in the week-by-week sections of this book.

I have never been very good at abstinence. I've often set myself the challenge of giving up my favourite sweet treats, but this abstinence can become hackneyed – a slimming diet, where cutting out sweets or chocolate takes the edges off the abundance we live in, but really benefits me only in a superficial way and is rewarded with a chocolate fest when I'm done. Any lasting impact is quickly forgotten – and that's on the occasions when I've actually managed not to give into temptation.

I feel I need to add a bit of perspective here, so you know where I'm coming from now and where I was coming from then. You see, my life has changed a lot since I did my challenge; almost beyond recognition in fact.

At the time, I was living a very well-off existence – definitely middle class, with a good job and a nice house in the London suburbs. I lived in a world of abundance, choice, and so much food. If there's a foodstuff that is actually unavailable in London, I don't know what it is, and I had not only the pick of British supermarkets on my doorstep, but also the pick of Asian, European, African, Latin American, and Middle Eastern foods within easy reach.

This made me into a self-professed foodie – to the point of gluttony. I was used to being able to pick what I wanted, when I wanted, and as much as I wanted. I've always loved trying new recipes, new restaurants, and exotic ingredients. I was generally too disorganized to make a packed lunch for work, so I'd nip out at lunchtime and grab whatever salad, sandwich, or pub lunch I fancied. It didn't really matter, because I could afford it and there was always more choice than you could ever get your head round.

These days, while I wouldn't class myself as poor, I certainly have to think of the budget constantly, and how to make it stretch. I now live in a very small town in a rural county, am self-employed, and earning roughly a third of what I earned when I did the challenge. Oh, and I have added two children to our household. In austere times, when everyone is tightening their belts and budgets, we are pretty much always making do and mending.

We're not the only ones, and we're most definitely not the worst off. Before we even get started on the Global South, there are so many people right here in the UK who are stretched to their limits trying to feed their families.

According to the Trussell Trust, a record number of people are accessing food banks in Britain right now. Their own food banks handed out three days' worth of food on over a million occasions between 1 April 2017 and 31 March 2018. Nearly half a million of those handouts went to children. Thankfully (and often thanks to kind friends and family) we've never reached the point of using food banks. But I know too many friends who have. It's a reality for a lot of people – and being hardworking and thrifty is not always enough to see you through.

I'm not complaining: I am living a life I chose. But when I first did the challenge, it was a voluntary break from the reality of my day-to-day existence. Now, the principles I discovered during my rationing are ones I have to apply as a matter of course. Questions of food, austerity, and waste are real and important ones. And I'm so grateful that I have some useful, applicable tools at hand; tools I got from doing this challenge.

As I progressed through the forty days, my challenge opened my eyes to more issues than I could have thought possible. Being restricted on what I could eat and drink showed me just how much we live in a global society, and the impact that our food choices have on people throughout the food supply chain.

As well as the lessons, the challenges of day-to-day living, and the local and national concerns I discovered, I realized that now more than ever it's important to know where our food comes from, how it's produced, and where we're letting down the people who put food on our plates.

The Fairtrade Foundation points out that by the time most of us have had breakfast, we've relied on half the world just to eat. But, more often than not, it's the half of the world that cannot feed its own people enough.

I had hoped that the challenge would make me much, much more conscious of what I have, what I waste, and what other people don't have. When you don't have unlimited access to food, food becomes an issue. I wasn't disappointed. This challenge was a journey for me – one of the most useful Lenten periods I have ever managed. By the end of it I had a new perspective on food, life and our relationship with God, our planet, and each other.

Please don't think that this challenge is purely about hardship! As I went through the Lenten period, armed with Marguerite Patten OBE's original wartime recipes, I discovered the real joy and triumph of being creative with very little. I found myself warming to the Blitz spirit attitude, the sense that "we're all in this together".

Because even though it might not be so obvious any more, that spirit still exists. Now more than ever, as we live as part of an increasingly global culture, our choices and actions have a ripple effect far beyond our own borders. As you'll see in the "Living on Rations" section, there are so many people who live by the "make do and mend" mantra. These people are often extraordinarily generous, motivated by a sense of community and a spirit of adventure.

Feeding a family, or friends, or yourself, on a dish that you've created from the bits and pieces you have to hand has a magic all of its own. The simple triumph of reaching the end of the week before you reach the end of the food is incredibly empowering.

If you take away anything from this book, I hope it's a sense of celebration: a sense that human beings have the wherewithal to overcome hardship and need. Through community, resourcefulness, and a sense of fun, even living on little can become a joyful thing.

The Rations Challenge:
Pre Week One

What the challenge is

Your challenge is simply to live on 1940s' rations for forty days. That means no imported food, and very restricted meat, dairy, and other food items. Hopefully, this book will provide you with the tools and inspiration to eat like a wartime Brit and, in actually changing your day-to-day habits, will give you an insight into some of the issues that still beset our food system and our world.

This section of the book is divided into daily bites. Each week, I start with a diary entry. These are my personal thoughts and experiences about living on rations, the questions it raised and the discoveries I made.

On Tuesday of every week, I'll be taking a look at the wartime kitchen – the contrasts between then and now, and whether or not we've improved on how people managed their food in the 1940s.

Wednesday leaves a little time for a pause: a chance to reflect on what the challenge might be throwing up for you, and a little quote to open yourself up to the ideas and thoughts surrounding your challenge and food in general.

Leading on from that, you can use Thursday as a chance to plant your feet in this topic. This is your book. Nobody will tell you off for scribbling in the margins or jotting down your ideas. Use today to think about where you stand and make a note of it if you like so you can look back and remind yourself of where you are today.

Towards the end of the week, there's a chance to "think global, act local". In 2015, the United Nations launched the Global Goals: fifteen goals designed to eradicate global hunger, waste, and inequality. Some of these goals go hand in hand with the rations challenge and thinking about how we can act to help these goals come to fruition.

So, having got a grasp on the issues, Saturday (perhaps the day you do your weekly shop?) gives you the opportunity to take that global knowledge and apply it to your own life, your food shop and your kitchen. None of it is rocket science; it absolutely doesn't need a big budget (in fact one of the happy side effects of doing the rations challenge is that you can save a whole lot of money on the grocery shop!) and it's unlikely to take any more footwork than usual to implement some positive changes. Nobody's expecting you to create a one-person revolution overnight. But it's nice to be part of the solution, isn't it?

And so you come to the end of the week. Sunday is a day of feasting. But while it is possible to create a slap-up family meal on rations (even if it's probably largely potato-based), these days are more about celebration, coming together, enjoying each other's company. Finishing each week with a little regroup with those we love is as important a part of this as anything we're doing with our carrot peelings.

So, onto the nitty-gritty! Having said all of the above, there are going to be some restrictions on what you can have, if you want to follow the challenge to the letter. On the next few pages, you'll find the complete rations sheet, and what this will mean for you over the next six weeks.

Good luck!

Claud Fullwood

What living on rations meant

A restricted diet: by 1943, milk, meat, cheese, butter, and fat were all rationed, as was sugar. Canned food and dry fruit were not rationed, but non-rationed food was restricted by market prices, or a points system. Each person had sixteen points per month. To put that in perspective, a tin of tomatoes would be roughly six points, and a tin of fruit was around twelve. You can see a full list of my rationed diet on the next page.

1. Seasonal and home-grown: no non-seasonal, non-British vegetables, because hardly any food was getting in by 1943. (Oh, Spam still got through from Canada apparently… it's debatable whether this is good news or not.) In the early months of the year, that means there's no fruit, and very few vegetables.

2. Planning ahead: although eating out wasn't rationed, it was restricted, and most people wouldn't have been able to afford to eat out very often. So "bye-bye" nipping out for a lunchtime baguette, and "hello" home-made soup! On days when I couldn't avoid eating out (I think I counted three occasions), I restricted myself to foods that would have been available at the time, and only one course.

3. Making do: I've always been a fan of the "make do and mend" ethos, it's just that I've never been that good at putting it into practice. Rationing certainly meant having to think and plan what you were going to eat.

When food isn't abundant, the time you spend thinking about it has to increase. Families had to economize during the war. They had to save and preserve in order to keep everyone fed – a far cry from our throwaway attitude today. This challenge is great for helping to focus on what we use, what we waste, and how to make food rations last.

How it worked: *the full ration sheet*

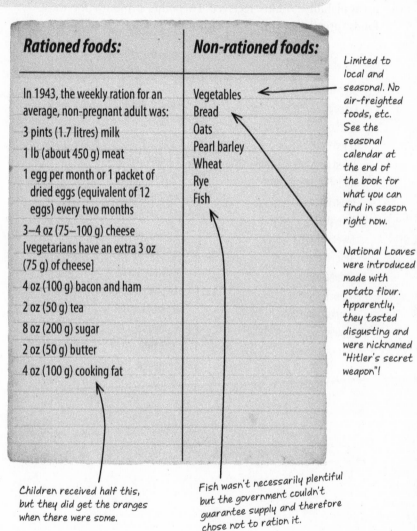

Rationed foods:

In 1943, the weekly ration for an average, non-pregnant adult was:

3 pints (1.7 litres) milk

1 lb (about 450 g) meat

1 egg per month or 1 packet of dried eggs (equivalent of 12 eggs) every two months

3–4 oz (75–100 g) cheese [vegetarians have an extra 3 oz (75 g) of cheese]

4 oz (100 g) bacon and ham

2 oz (50 g) tea

8 oz (200 g) sugar

2 oz (50 g) butter

4 oz (100 g) cooking fat

Non-rationed foods:

Vegetables

Bread

Oats

Pearl barley

Wheat

Rye

Fish

Limited to local and seasonal. No air-freighted foods, etc. See the seasonal calendar at the end of the book for what you can find in season right now.

National Loaves were introduced made with potato flour. Apparently, they tasted disgusting and were nicknamed "Hitler's secret weapon"!

Children received half this, but they did get the oranges when there were some.

Fish wasn't necessarily plentiful but the government couldn't guarantee supply and therefore chose not to ration it.

Other food was rationed on a points-based system, subject to availability. Adults received 16 points a month for these foods (usually tinned). Points for some foods are as follows:

British tinned fruit	24 points per lb (450 g)
Cereals	4 points per lb
Crackers	2 points per lb
Dried fruit	8 points per lb
Dried peas/beans/lentils, etc.	4 points per lb
Imported tinned fruit	12 points per lb
Plain biscuits	2 points per lb
Rice/pasta	8 points per lb
Sweet biscuits	4 points per lb
Tinned beans/peas	4 points per lb
Tinned meat	8 points per lb
Tinned salmon/tuna	16 points per lb
Tinned tomatoes	6 points per lb
Golden syrup/black treacle	4 points per lb
Sausage meat	12 points per lb (rationed 1943–45)

WEEK ONE:

What Happened to My Unlimited Choice?

Monday: diary entry week one

This week, I'm eating a *lot* of potatoes. As one of my few "free" foods, they've formed the basis of most of my meals so far, including breakfast, for which I've been eating the delightfully named "fadge" – a sort of griddled potato cake a bit like a hash brown (much, much tastier than the name suggests).

I didn't think I had a limit for potato eating; the last roastie is always what gets fought over in our house. But, by day four, I woke up feeling slightly queasy at the thought of another round of fadge, so I switched to water-based porridge instead and sprinkled a bit of my sugar ration on the top. Who knew that grey mush would feel like such a treat?!

I'm finding the sugar ration an interesting one. As sugar beet was a big crop in Britain during wartime, the weekly ration was 8 oz (225 g) which seems pretty generous to me. Certainly it looks like the biggest bit of food in the ration box. Unfortunately, because I don't have sugar in tea and tend not to have it in cereal (although I've appreciated it on my porridge, now lacking the extra sweetness of milk), it's not a whole lot of use to me. With so little milk and butter and virtually no egg, I'd need to save up my weekly and monthly rations of everything else to do what I'd normally do with that much sugar, which is bake with it.

The thing I'm noticing the most is a radical cutback on choice. As a very spoilt westerner, my biggest struggle is that every meal is a variation on the same few ingredients. This was never going to be a starvation diet, and I've definitely got enough to eat. But it is bringing home powerfully the thought that, as soon as food is scarce, choice becomes a luxury. What I'm beginning to understand is: living where I do gives me an incredible amount of choice. And most of my choices – certainly where food is concerned – are pleasurable ones. But food, like any other resource, needs to be approached with moderation and common sense. There's only enough to go around if we don't demand unlimited choice.

Every human being has choices to make. For some, those choices are life and death, for others, a luxury. I'm not saying we should live on potatoes; this would not help anyone, and the outbreaks of scurvy would put a lot of strain on the National Health Service. But we can choose to be responsible, to waste less, and to do more with what we have.

Having a global food system isn't a bad thing: countries with farming economies rely on being able to export their coffee, bananas, avocados, and all the other foods that often make up a weekly average shopping basket. And I absolutely appreciate the joy of being able to experience foods from around the world; what a wonder and a privilege that is.

It's also not a choice between supporting local or supporting global. The more we make intelligent choices about using local produce, the more we free up space to make responsible choices about what we consume from overseas. Far from standing in opposition to each other, buying local and global produce very much goes hand in hand.

Making good choices when sourcing our food is essential. We can recognize that if we want to drink fresh ground coffee or buy beautiful, sweet, yellow bananas (boy, am I missing those right now!), then there is a perceived cost and an actual cost. By checking for a Fairtrade mark, we're making a good choice for everyone in that chain.

We're not stuck with the system we have. We can choose justice for everyone.

Tuesday: then and now

Then

It pretty much goes without saying that choice was a rare commodity in the wartime kitchen. So, the focus was very much on being creative with what you had.

I love those wartime recipes which helped cooks to substitute what they had to do without: eggless cakes, fatless sponges. How brilliant that rationed Britons went to such lengths to create so much with the small amounts of ingredients they had!

Cooks and food writers were so resourceful with the very unexciting rations sheet. As well as treats, recipes for curried carrots, potato bread and mock cream, they even devised "orange juice" made from carrots – because where would you see an actual orange at that time? And even if you managed to find one, they were reserved for children.

The rationed diet was limited, but it was balanced. It had all the nutrients necessary to be healthy, and despite food shortages, Britain did not go hungry.

Now

Britain imports food from all over the world and has access to an almost unlimited number of fruits, vegetables, delicacies, and specialities. Yet the amount of fruit and veg we eat in the UK today is actually falling – most of us don't even manage the recommended minimum of five portions a day, and it's estimated that we throw away around a fifth of the fruit and veg we buy.[1] We have more choice, but we don't seem to make good choices.

As a result, the energy we get from food these days has been on a downward trajectory since 2001.[2] A bit scary to think that, while we have so much more to choose from, we are self-restricting our energy intake more now than rationing ever did. And sad to think that we're throwing away the incredible abundance living in a global society gifts us with!

Wednesday: *time to reflect*

"Your power to choose can never be taken from you. It can be neglected and it can be ignored. But if used, it can make all the difference."[3]

Steve Goodier (author, Methodist minister, and motivational speaker)

Thursday: where do I stand?

It's Thursday of the first week and, if you're doing the challenge, you're probably missing some foods you'd normally enjoy.

Find a pencil and take yourself to a quiet spot. Use the space below to write a list of food you're missing: foods that aren't available locally or on the rations sheet. Allow yourself a few minutes to really appreciate what they add to your weekly meals, what kinds of taste, texture, and interest they bring.

The idea is not to torture yourself with what you're missing! But it's useful to create an awareness of what being part of a global food system can really add to our plates – and what *we* can bring to or take away from the lives of others.

Take a moment to be glad for the connections we have with the wider world, and maybe jot down a few ways to make sure, when your challenge is over, that you can make good choices for everyone in the food supply chain.

Think about:
- What labels do you want to pay attention to?
- Who can you support through your choices?
- What food is best for you and/or your family?

Friday: think global

In Britain, we import just under half of our food from overseas, and three quarters of our fruit and veg. So, it's pretty clear that we rely on a substantial chunk of the world for our daily bread. But not all imported food is created equal.[4]

In the UK, we drink 95 million cups of coffee a day.[5]

But so many of the farmers who supply the beans live in the kind of poverty which means skipping meals for months on end.[6]

UN Global Goal #8:
Achieve decent work and economic growth[9]

- *Sustainable inclusive economic growth*
- *Full and productive employment*
- *Equal pay for equal work, decent working conditions, supporting small businesses*
- *Eradicate the worst forms of unfair labour*

Buying fairly traded products puts money into the hands of the people and communities who earned it.[8]

They watch their children suffer from malnutrition because they're not paid a fair price for their product[7]

Saturday: act local

At the moment, you may not feel so in touch with global food markets, beyond picking up strawberries in the supermarket and sadly putting them back when you see they're from Morocco.

Try to choose supermarkets that have good ethical reputations. They're not always the most expensive.

Take this time to become more aware of the "food world" around you and put some good habits together for now and the future.

Where you can, buy locally grown produce; where you can't, make it fair.

Get to know what food really costs to produce. Talk to suppliers here and use that knowledge when you go back to buying imported food.

Choose seasonal. It tastes better! When you can have imported food again, check it's in season where it comes from.

Think about what you really need: just because we can buy everything, doesn't mean we need it all at once. Let the rations challenge shape how you shop; only buy what you can use.

Sunday: feast

Why not use this Sunday to come together with family or friends? Your food choices may be limited but there are so many other choices you still have!

Choose to put your phones, tablets, and screens away; spend time talking and catching up about your week.

Why not start an adventure tin? Have everyone write down some things they'd like to do together as a family or group of friends and then pick one out at random. You could keep the tin topped up throughout your challenge and beyond. It's always a good day for an adventure!

Of course, during the war, family activities and games would have looked quite different from how they look today; it's up to you whether you choose new or vintage. Here are a few ideas for wartime fun you might want to include:

- A family walk
- Play board games
- Go on a foraging expedition: what's in season now? You might even make the rations stretch a bit more! Make sure you take a reliable book or guide, especially if you're looking for berries or mushrooms.
- Make a toy or game out of recycled materials from your house (in true *Blue Peter* style!). Draw or paint a board onto a big piece of paper, use bottle tops for counters... then play away for the afternoon. NB: not having kids around is no excuse not to get in touch with your inner child...

WEEK TWO:
Waste and Landfill

Monday: diary entry week two

Before the rations challenge, I hadn't thought much about what I *needed*, only what I'd *like* to eat. So I've often ended up throwing food out (guiltily, expecting my super-saver mum to burst in yelling *"No-o-o-o-o!"* in a slow-motion fashion) because I bought too much.

Now, I'm working out how to make food stretch, and appreciating how my own mum and gran had to balance everything to feed their big families. And the food waste is disappearing! The most I throw away is carrot tops and leek bottoms. I've stopped peeling carrots and spuds (a good scrub does as well and wastes less; also I've heard there are good nutrients in the skins that are lost if you peel). With the meat, cheese and milk rations, I work out what I need each day and how to make it last. It's a revelation.

The wartime approach to waste was an absolute homage to good sense and good housekeeping. The Ministry of Food used propaganda to encourage less waste at home, producing recipes which showed how to use every scrap of rationed food with minimal waste, with the Food Advice Division giving demonstrations in public places to show how to use rations wisely. Everyone was encouraged to grow their own food; every garden was a potential vegetable plot. In fact, food became so important during the Second World War, that if you were caught wasting food you could be prosecuted.

It might be hard to believe, but Britain hadn't been a thrifty, home-growing paragon of virtue before war broke out. Before the Second World War, only a third of our food was home-grown and clearly the Ministry of Food had to work hard to convince people how to cook, eat, and reduce their waste once it became imperative. Such a huge emphasis was placed on waste in wartime propaganda that it must have been something that hadn't really entered peoples' consciousness much before.

This should be a comfort to us now: in the space of just a few years, food waste was cut so dramatically as to be virtually non-existent. So, when we look at the vast food waste that our society generates now, we don't need to despair. It might look like a pipe dream to pull back from our landfill habits but, if the war tells us anything, it is that applying the right kind of pressure in the right places can yield great changes in a short space of time.

I'm not talking about starting a war just so we all straighten up and fly right. There are plenty of important reasons to stop food waste now, without the threat of war! And although there were penalties for food waste, much of the wartime propaganda didn't focus on threatening people into submission. The emphasis was instead on being part of a community, doing your bit: digging for victory and also the satisfaction to be had from living sustainably. Which of us doesn't love that feel-good factor?

The Ministry of Food may have used propaganda, but that doesn't mean they were telling lies (unlike the *Saucepans for Spitfires* campaign – it turns out you can't actually turn aluminium pans into fighter jets). The massive effort the British people made to survive on less, waste less, and make do more, was a driving factor in winning the war.

The same spirit can help us win the war on want and waste today.

Tuesday: then and now

Then

While it's true that, during the war, wasting food was an offence, the positive side of the Ministry of Food's campaign was that thousands of Britons got on board with the "Dig for Victory" drive. By the end of the war, Britain had become an example of efficiency and self-reliance.

Neighbourhood "pig clubs" were set up, adding thousands of tonnes of pork to peoples' rations and providing a clever use for household scraps and peelings. Some councils set up public food waste bins, collecting food scraps to send to farms.[10]

More and more people were digging for victory. Front and back gardens were turned into vegetable plots, and in the cities, sections of public parks (including Kensington Gardens and even the grounds of the Tower of London) were portioned into allotments so that city folk could do their bit.[11] By 1943, home gardens were producing an estimated 1 million tonnes of food per year. And by the end of the war, there were 1,300,000 allotments in Britain.[12]

Now

Seven million tonnes of food are thrown away from our homes each year – and most of it could have been eaten.[13]

On the plus side, there are campaigns afoot to turn food waste into food resource, looking at every aspect of the supply chain for ways to cut waste.

The number of people keeping chickens at home is on the rise. It's estimated that over 600,000 households in Britain now keep chickens, as more and more people return to the *Good Life* values.[14] Not only does this supply an extra food source but feeding scraps to chickens also helps keep household food waste down.

As people become more concerned about food miles and waste, allotments are also becoming popular again. There are around 250,000 allotments in the UK and an additional 90,000 people (as of 2018) are on waiting lists.[15] And of course this doesn't include the many people like us who have portioned off their gardens – or set up window boxes or balcony pots – to grow vegetables at home. I've come to believe that there is nothing that tastes as good as the food you bring in and cook from your own garden.

Wednesday: time to reflect

"When they had all had enough to eat, he said to his disciples, 'Gather the pieces that are left over. Let nothing be wasted.' So they gathered them and filled twelve baskets with the pieces of the five barley loaves left over by those who had eaten."

John 6:12–13 (NIV)

Thursday: where do I stand?

Find a quiet place. Think of the food you have in your home right now. Pick one item to focus on. Either using the space below, or just in your head, create a map of how that food got to your table.

Have a guess at how many people and processes it has taken to bring that item to your table. How much of it will you use? What will you do with any leftovers? How can you do your part to minimize waste and want?

*Let's take a moment to be thankful
for the producers who bring
the food to our tables.*

Friday: think global

One third of the 4 billion metric tonnes of food produced on earth is lost or wasted. And this at a time when one in eight people are hungry.

Smaller producers
= less waste.

Better storage
systems, silos, etc.
= less food loss.

Redistributing
surplus food to food
banks and outreach
groups all helps to
save waste.

UN Global Goal #12:

Responsible consumption and production[16]

- *Sustainable management of natural resources*
- *Halve global food waste across the supply and consumption chain*
- *Manage chemicals and minimize environmental impact*

Cutting waste and
feeding hungry
people = bureaucracy
at its best.

CHOOSING UGLY
SAVES WASTE!
Supermarkets sell conformity.
But knobbly tomatoes and two-
headed mushrooms mean less
waste and often more taste.

One fifth of everything we throw away is useable, but the labels can often be confusing. New labelling regulations should save waste. In France, recent laws ban supermarkets from throwing out useable food. They have to donate it to food banks.

Saturday: act local

The food revolution starts
in your fridge! Here are
some tips for cutting your
waste – and making your
rations last! Here are tips
I've gathered from my
experience and research.

Work with the use-by
dates. If something's going
off soon, use it first. Stock rotate
your fridge, but don't just go by
the use-by date. Sure, use-by
dates shouldn't be treated lightly,
but remember if you buy loose
vegetables they often don't have a
use-by date anyway. And "sell-by"
and "best before" dates are nothing
more than recommendations.
Use touch, smell, and – if it's
safe – taste to see if your
food is past its best.

Save your storage. Save glass
jars and sealable food packaging
where you can to store
leftovers. You'll cut your cling
film use and be less likely to
chuck stuff away.

Plan creatively. When you cook, plan what you can turn your leftovers into. You'll save money and time, and definitely cut your waste.

Portion up in advance. If you find yourself throwing out half of the pre-packaged food you buy, plan ahead. Put half your loaf in the freezer, or make a large batch of stew and divide it. Bingo: two nights' dinner in one!

Clear out the cupboards and use up what you find. Great for cutting waste and you can let your inner master chef loose creating a feast from oddments! The downside: when you make something amazing, you'll never remember what you put in it!

Become a salvage superhero. Turn stale bread into croutons, meat bones into gravy. Save your vegetable scraps (carrot and parsnip tops, onion and leek ends, herb stems, etc) in the freezer. When you have a bagful, put it in a pot and cover it with water, simmer for two hours and strain. Homemade vegetable stock!

Make soup. The best and easiest way to use whatever's in the fridge. Throw it in a pan with some water or stock. Boil it up. Whizz it up if you like. Eat it.

35

Sunday: feast

Make a leftover lunch
What's the most creative Sunday dinner you can create from this week's portions? Involve the family: who can come up with the most inventive, least wasteful use of what's in the fridge?

Have a make do and mend afternoon
Gather up all those cardigans with lost buttons and possessions you've been thinking of throwing out because they're broken. I'll bet that, if you set aside some time, you can give them a new lease of life without spending any money. If you have handy friends, invite them round and get them to teach you how to do it!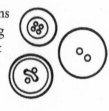

Go *Blue Peter*
Before you throw all the packaging in the bin, could you re-purpose it into something beautiful? Get the kids involved, get creative... there are thousands if not millions of ways to use an empty washing-up bottle and a kitchen roll tube on the internet. Fill your house with free, unique art.

Organize a swap shop
One person's trash is another's treasure... and by far the most environmentally friendly, low-waste way to recycle is to gather your friends, and neighbours and then "swap it". Everybody brings stuff they don't need or want and hopefully goes home with an item they've always wanted.

WEEK THREE:

What our Mums Have Taught Us

Monday: diary entry week three

•

One of my most treasured possessions is my Kenwood stand mixer – a legacy kitchen piece which belonged to both of my grandmothers and my mum before I got it. It weighs about half a tonne. Judging from the weight of it, it must be made of cast iron and Bakelite, very possibly painted with some kind of lead-based paint, and despite being well over sixty years old, runs as sweet as a nut.

I think about the generations of barmbracks, birthday cakes, and biscuits which have sallied forth from its dented steel mixing bowl, and I'm convinced my own cakes taste all the better because of it.

My lovely gran lived through the war and rationing, and so was a goldmine of information and help. Like her own mum, she was great at making supplies stretch, despite (also like her mum) having an abundance of children – both her own and those that she fostered.

"There wasn't much bread," she said, "but we made soda bread. And for stew you could sometimes get a bone from the butcher. It was a good idea to make friends with the butcher, and then he'd put aside an extra bone for you to boil."

Gran was a charmer; the butcher never stood a chance. But she gave far more than she got and she was a fierce and caring friend. "We looked after each other," she told me. "Neighbours helped neighbours and we shared what we had. That's how it worked."

This marvel of scrimping, sharing and soda bread is my legacy. I grew up in a home where "waste not, want not" hung in the air alongside aromas of bubble and squeak. From Gran, my mum learned how to make her food budget stretch and feed her own big family.

It's a standing joke that if you gave my mum an old boot and an empty tin can, she'd turn it into a nutritious meal for eight people. Mum's ability to make do and mend kept us all in shoes, coats (usually hand-me-downs) and healthy dinners (albeit generally leftovers). We tease her for saving a spoonful of leftover peas in a ramekin in the fridge after Sunday lunch, but the truth is she's bang-on about using up leftovers and making food stretch. We never went hungry, and neither did anyone else who turned up with a rumbling tum.

Here are some things I've learned from my mum, and my mum's mum:

1. Sunday leftovers are Monday's dinner.
2. Never throw anything away. Look at what you've got in the fridge and see what you can do with it.
3. The best soda bread recipe ever (find it in the "Wartime Cookery" section; enjoy it with your bit of rationed cheese).
4. Use the whole lot. If you've had a roast chicken on Sunday, boil up the bones for stock, because that's free gravy or soup base and it tastes a whole world better than gravy granules.
5. An onion and a tablespoon of oil can turn any collection of random food into a dinner.
6. Bulk out the tasty bits: using potatoes, pearl barley, oats, rice and pasta (although be careful about these last two if you're on wartime rations) makes meat and veg go a whole lot further.

Tuesday: then and now

Then

As we know, the wartime generation of women worked wonders to hold Britain together, keeping the country in food, and did countless other acts of service that they're only in recent years starting to get recognition for.

Women with bottle

The Ministry of Food appointed the Women's Institute (WI) to teach Brits how to bottle, preserve, and pickle surplus fruit and veg. Five thousand WI preservation centres were set up countrywide so WI volunteers could collect fruit that could not be used by growers or transported. Between 1940 and 1945, they preserved over 5,300 tonnes of fruit – the equivalent of a year's jam ration for more than half a million people.[17]

Heroines of the home front

The Women's Voluntary Service (WVS) was set up in June 1938, aiming to recruit 30,000 volunteers to the Air Raid Precautions services, the Civil Nursing Reserve and Hospital Supply Depots, and as ambulance drivers.[18] By the outbreak of war in September 1939, the WVS had 300,000 members, who helped wherever needed. They helped organize city evacuations, emergency clothing distribution, and worked through the Blitz in emergency kitchens to keep firemen fed and victims sheltered. After D-Day, the WVS went to Europe to help troops there as well.

Land Girls

The Women's Land Army, set up in 1939, recruited "Land Girls" aged seventeen and over from city and country alike. By 1944, it had over 80,000 members.[19] These brilliant women were sent to work in all areas of farming and were largely responsible for keeping Britain fed while male farm workers went overseas. See Peggy's story in the "Living on Rations" section for a first-hand account of life as a Land Girl.

By the end of the war, 7 million women were in work, many in traditionally masculine jobs such as munitions factories and auxiliary armed forces.[20] But, after the war, women stepped aside for the returning men and, by 1951, the number of women in work had returned to pre-war levels. The Women's Land Army continued until 1950 to help with food shortages.

Now

Not just jam and Jerusalem

Over 100 years after it was founded, the WI has around 220,000 members in 6,300 WIs.[21] As well as offering its members a massive variety of social, sport and cultural activities, the WI is still an active campaigning platform. Lobbying on everything from climate change and the plight of the honey bee to equal pay and more midwives, the WI is a loud and well-informed voice on current issues.

In 2016, they produced a resolution calling upon supermarkets to sign an agreement to cut food waste and pass their surplus stock onto charities for redistribution.

And yes, they still make great jam.

The WVS is now the Royal Voluntary Service. These days, some 32,000 volunteers still run services for elderly people, such as Meals on Wheels, visiting and befriending, running hospital shops, and organizing community transport to help people get out and about.

The women of the Second World War sowed the seeds for gender equality, and over the next few decades, women achieved equal working rights, equal pay, and the outlawing of sex discrimination. There's still a way to go – especially on a global scale – but thanks to those brilliant women paving the way, we may get there yet.

Wednesday: time to reflect

Why Shouldn't She?

My mother loved cooking
but hated washing up
Why shouldn't she?
cooking was an art
she could move her lips to
then the pleasure
feeding the proverbial
multitude (us)
on less than a loaf
and two fishes

**by Grace Nichols, *The Fat Black Woman's Poems*,
Virago Poets (1984)**

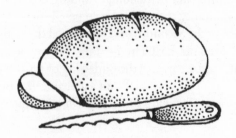

Thursday: where do I stand?

Find a quiet place for ten minutes. Turn off your phone. Plant your feet squarely so you can feel the earth beneath you and your connection to it. Breathe.

Imagine you are part of a chain: a line of wisdom and experiences passed down.

Whether it's obvious, like a family proverb you often repeat, or more hidden but ingrained, like those traditions which are so much part of life you've forgotten they're traditions, you have inherited so much of who you are from the generations before you.

This week, we have been honouring the unique contribution of women both to heritage and to the war effort. What have you inherited from the women in your family? What did they teach you?

What have you kept to pass on to the next generation?

From the wartime generation, we learn many arts that sadly seem to be dying: neighbourliness, self-sacrifice, fairness, resourcefulness, inclusion.

Friday: think global

Gender equality is a human right. But it's still a dream for a lot of women around the world.[22]

- Worldwide, women are still much more likely than men to be poor and illiterate.
- They're less likely to have jobs, get training or own property.
- They're often denied access to political systems and are still far more likely to be victims of domestic violence than men.

But when women are empowered – when they have more influence, better education, more independence, and autonomy – families, communities, and whole nations benefit. More often than not the benefits are passed on to the next generation.

Infant and maternal mortality rates drop.[23]

Empowering women leads to healthier, wealthier, happier, and more productive societies.[24]

When women are educated, their children tend to have better prospects.[25]

In many companies, clearing a path for women to get into the workforce has proven to cut staff turnover and increase stability.[26]

Closing the gender gap would make really big changes in economic growth, especially in ageing populations where the workforce is shrinking.[27]

UN Global Goal #5:
Achieve gender equality for all women and girls

- *End discrimination and violence against all women and girls.*
- *Ensure women can participate equally and become leaders at all levels of decision-making in public life.*
- *Give women equal rights to economic resources, access to ownership of and control over land and property, financial services, inheritance, and natural resources.*

Saturday: act local

While the men were fighting on the frontlines in World War Two, women were fighting the war on the home front. What an amazing legacy we've inherited from a whole generation!

Now, men *and* women are fighting in our armed forces around the world. Wouldn't it be great if they didn't have to?

Everyone, both women and men, can move for positive change in our own society and beyond. What will our legacy be to the next generation? How will we bear witness to the injustices in our world?

Volunteer

Whether you're coaching a rugby team, running a youth group, helping out at a shelter or volunteering at your local school, by giving your time, you're giving a huge gift. And if you can't commit that much, how about looking into micro-volunteering? Small acts of kindness in under ten minutes: big changes.

Campaign

If you see something that needs fixing, shout about it. You can lobby your local MP or join a campaign from a charity or group. So often ordinary people come together and make extraordinary strides forward: on poverty, inequality, violence and discrimination.

Be a role model

Everyone has something to pass on. It could be a skill, an experience, or just the example we set by the way we treat others.

Sunday: feast

Make time for mum

Make time with your mum – or someone whose love, care and wisdom makes them special to you. Organize a dinner, or just give them a call and let them know you're thinking of them.

Have a "bring and share" dinner

When you're on rations you might not feel you have much to share. But if everyone brings a little bit to share, watch how it multiplies.

Learn a lost art

You probably know someone in the older generation who has some serious skills, be it planting tomatoes, knitting, or fixing a leaking tap. Take the opportunity to learn from them. Learning new skills is something you'll never regret or forget.

WEEK FOUR:

*Living Below
the Breadline —
Food Banks and
Austerity Budgets*

Monday: diary entry week four

As I may have already groaned, I'm finding the monotony of rations a chore to deal with. I'm used to variety, and this regime lacks inspiration. Frankly, I'm bored. If only I kept chickens! A few more eggs would be wonderful right now, not to mention a bit of extra meat. *[When I did this challenge, I was pretty clueless about seasonal cooking. But it turns out it's a bit of an adventure. Find tips and recipes in the final section of the book.]*

But I have to admit, I am eating pretty healthily. If you're living on rations, you can't eat too much fat or sugar, and there's not much I can fill up my plate with except those "free" foods. On the whole, this means vegetables and more vegetables. *[Actually, there is a huge variety of vegetables grown in the UK all year round. If you need some inspiration, have a look at the seasonal calendar at the end of the book.]*

The principles behind rationing were founded not only on making do and home-grown, but also on proper nutrition. The government realized that there must be enough food for everyone, and that the food needed to be balanced and nutritious. It was a policy which cared and catered for poor people in a way we rarely see in society today.

The Ministry of Food wasn't only interested in making sure the food lasted. They understood that for everyone to stay healthy, everyone had to have a fair share.

As such, the very wealthy had to get used to eating only their share, so that the very poor could keep going. Put another way, the rich had to live more simply, so the poor could simply live.

The other part to the plan was education. It wasn't enough just to ration food: the Ministry saw that people needed educating about nutrition. As Marguerite Patten OBE put it: "I am sure it was during the war years that the British learned how to cook vegetables correctly, so they retained flavour, colour, and texture plus valuable mineral salts and vitamins."[28]

I don't for a moment think that the wartime government was any more compassionate or big-hearted than any other government. Food wasn't free (except relief food in bombed areas) and, of course, the wealthy still fared better than the poor. But the government showed a great deal of common sense: we needed "all hands on deck" and we needed people to be fit for work. The last thing the government wanted was a malnourished workforce.

But… isn't that the same issue today? Some countries in the world are unable to develop because their people don't have enough to eat. Because food is unavailable, prices are high, markets are unstable, and that leaves no money for education or essential services. People become weak and sick, which decimates the workforce. In our own country, and throughout the Western world, the very poorest people are malnourished and often become sick because of poor diet.

And this is a travesty, because there is enough food to go around. If people are well-fed and healthy, we know beyond doubt that they have the resourcefulness, creativity, and drive to lift entire nations out of poverty.

I think we're ready for change; I think we're hungry for it. I think we need to keep questioning and questioning: why food isn't being shared out properly; why people's most basic needs are being held to ransom for profit; why I get to choose whether or not to use food carefully. The wartime ethos of "we're all in this together" needs reinstating, but not just on a national scale. We have one world: one finite, albeit abundant resource. We are *all* in this together, across the globe. It's time to get global on global hunger.

Tuesday: then and now

Then

The carefully balanced nutrition of the rations sheet went hand in hand with educating the population about food and cooking.

Potato Pete's recipe book

Food demonstrations, often carried out by WI volunteers, along with leaflets and even friendly vegetable characters (Potato Pete and his friend, Dr Carrot) were used to help people really make their rations stretch.

By the end of the war, Britain was a savvy nation regarding nutrition, with children actually growing bigger and stronger than in pre-war years, and infant mortality rates dropping markedly. Under rations, we all started living longer.

Although rations weren't free, fair food prices made them easier to access for poor families. With the emphasis on creating your own vegetable gardens, learning how to cook efficiently, and avoid waste, and so much public information, the system was pretty successful.

"We'll have lots to eat this winter, won't we Mother?"

Grow your own
Can your own

Ministry of Food propaganda was nothing short of brilliant. Boosting morale, enabling and empowering families to take control of their rations: this was a key part to making it all work.

Now

Sadly, it seems Britain is in a food crisis once again. The Trussell Trust reports that use of its food banks is at an all-time high, with over a million three-day emergency food packs being given out each year. [29]

The top reasons for using food banks are not only low income, but also delays in receiving essential benefits and allowances. The sad truth is that many people in the UK live on a tightrope, and the slightest wobble can tip them towards food poverty.

Research also shows that it's not only people who are unemployed who are falling on hard times and having to rely on the kindness of strangers. In these austere times, many people who are in employment are experiencing new levels of hardship, as their hours are cut, or their contracts changed. The rug is pulled out from under them.

Meanwhile, packaging on our food now gives us a great deal of information on nutritional value – how much fat, salt, and sugar it contains, and how many calories. We can see where our food comes from and it's easier to follow the food chain.

But is this really helping ordinary people make choices about food? Is it the right information in the right place? And is the packaging itself making food more expensive than it needs to be, and more wasteful than it should be? Would more people benefit from word-of-mouth demonstrations, just as the WI provided during the Second World War? How do we get the right education and information to people who need it?

Food banks are charitable institutions and they do amazing work. In addition to helping people in times of crisis, it's often charities like the Trussell Trust which open up conversations about what we, as a country, can do to stop food crises. Right now, this includes bringing the voices of people living in food poverty to the ears of those in power, and opening up a conversation everyone can get involved in.

Wednesday: *time to reflect*

"There are people in the world so hungry, that God cannot appear to them except in the form of bread."

Mahatma Gandhi (Civil rights activist and leader of Indian independence movement)

Thursday: where do I stand?

This week, you could find a quiet place to contemplate – or, if you prefer, maybe find a spot to watch the world go by: sit on a park bench or stroll down your local high street.

Feel how you are part of a wider community: surrounded by people with busy, often difficult lives.

How many people do you know? How many lives are touching yours? Think about the people you meet through your job, your church or community group, your hobbies.

You are part of a wide community of individuals and families. What do you know of the people who surround you?

Are there people who have offered you support or help in times of need? Or people you have done that for?

Take time to open your eyes and ears to your community. Maybe you know of people who may be struggling now.

A sympathetic ear or a helping hand in the right place can truly be a saving grace to people in need.

Take a moment to think about – and perhaps write down – some instances where people have shown that help to you.

How can we show love and enable dignity when someone is in trouble?

Friday: think global

There are almost seven billion people on this planet. And one in nine of us doesn't have enough to eat. But there's definitely enough food to go around. So why are people hungry?

Poverty trap
Put simply: if you can't afford food, you get weak and sick. If you're weak and sick, you're less likely to be able to earn enough to escape poverty.

Lack of investment in agriculture
As well as land and seed, growing food takes roads, storage, and irrigation. Investing in agriculture reduces food poverty more effectively than investing in other types of industry.[30]

Climate
Increasing natural disasters (floods, storms, drought) are bad news for hungry people, causing crop failures and death of livestock. Climate change and deforestation also add to soil erosion – on land that could be used for food.

War and displacement
Food production gets abandoned when people are forced to flee a country because of war. Food becomes a weapon: armies starve the other side by cutting off food supplies, destroying markets, planting landmines in fields, or poisoning water wells.

Unstable markets
Price spikes and unstable food markets can put some food groups out of reach for the world's poorest people. Having to rely on cheaper, less nutritious foods can lead to malnutrition, especially in small children.

Waste!

One third of all food produced is never consumed, and producing it guzzles up natural resources vital for feeding the planet. It also adds 3.3 billion tonnes of greenhouse gases to the atmosphere, with consequences for the climate and, ultimately, food production.[31]

Saturday: act local

Get to know your neighbours!

One fifth of UK households experiences some level of food poverty. Which means: if it isn't you, it's likely to be someone you know. Here are some ways to help meet the needs in your own community:

- Volunteering at your local shelter or community centre, or even serving tea and coffee at a church service or social inclusion group. Go with friends and family and it can be great fun!
- If time is precious, maybe you can squeeze in a drop-off of a food donation at your nearest food bank. Drop-off points tend to be at supermarkets, community centres, and churches; why not find out where your nearest one is?
- Are there people in your community who struggle to get to the shops? Could you volunteer to pick up a neighbour's groceries when you fetch yours?
- Check out what food charities and other organizations are helping out in your town. There's always someone who could use a helping hand.
- Admitting to struggling is not always the easiest thing for people to do, and so many families become isolated in addition to struggling with food. Keep your ears and eyes open to people who may be in need, but less able to admit it.
- Organize a "real junk food" dinner: use up leftovers and good food destined for the bin to put on a dinner for people going without.

Sunday: feast

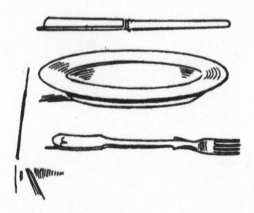

Make a place at your table today.

Why not make space for someone you wouldn't usually invite? In keeping with your rations challenge, you can make it a simple lunch, perhaps using up your leftovers.

If the spirit of friendship and community is present, any food becomes tastier!

WEEK FIVE:

Local Versus Imported — Eating Seasonally and Sustainably

Monday: diary entry week five

I'm well into the swing of rations these days. I'm becoming a dab hand at knocking up a few wholemeal scones and making sure I divvy up my protein for each day – and I can murder a potato in any one of a dozen devilish ways.

Meanwhile my grocery bills are down, and my waste is down... even my waist seems to be benefiting from this restriction (and if ever there was a sign that I have far too much, it's that I see a weight reduction as a bonus).

Maybe I'm writing on a good day – one where the thought of one more potato doesn't make me weep – but my thoughts for today are: it's really not so bad. A few more eggs, and I reckon I'd be happy to adopt it on a longer-term basis. Oh, and some tomatoes. And oranges... and the occasional avocado.

OK, there are definitely things I miss. But the benefit of the ration regime is that it really lets you get to grips with what's essential and what's a luxury. And the fact is, I've got all the essentials.

I wonder if I'd appreciate lots of things more if I only ate them seasonally. Most of us rarely consider if our fruit and veg is seasonal these days because you can always get what you want. But if we always get the season's best it not only tastes better, we also become by default more aware and responsible shoppers.

Here's one important lesson I'll be taking forward from the challenge: overseas food is a luxury which adds variety and excitement to my diet. And, if I get seasonal, local produce where I can, I will most likely have enough money to get my overseas produce from sustainable, responsible sources.

I don't want to stop buying avocados, and oranges, and bananas, not least because overseas producers do, after all, rely on that trade. But I want to see those extra luxuries for what they are: gifts and privileges – and, therefore, not to be bought carelessly or for knockdown prices.

Food that comes from overseas represents people's livelihoods, every bit as much as buying carrots from Hereford is supporting farmers here. So not taking responsibility for whom I buy from should no longer be an option.

It's not right that people don't get a fair price for what they produce, here or overseas. But what a magical thought it is that buying power could mean the end to both poverty and waste.

Buying Fairtrade means growers today get a good deal, and big companies have to think a bit harder about their supply chains. Taking action to change the food system for good might mean that in years to come, we'll be able to shake our heads in disbelief at the idea that fairly traded food was ever a choice we got to make.

And while I can't get my overseas produce to jazz up my dinners, eating local doesn't have to be boring! Even in slower seasons there is plenty to work with, and by eating more seasonally you can really get in touch with what your body needs most.

Just looking at a seasonal calendar (like the one at the end of this book) will open your eyes to just how much abundance there is on the home front. With a little creativity you can find ways to serve up a feast, even in the middle of January, on wartime rations.

Tuesday: then and now

Then

At the start of the war in 1939, Britain imported around 70 per cent of its food per year, including nearly all of its cheese, sugar, fruit, cereals, and fats.[31] Even vegetables like onions which, of course, can easily be grown in our climate.

The UK also imported more than half of its meat as well as feed to support its domestic meat production. No wonder the Axis powers decided to attack British shipping routes and starve Britain into submission!

By the end of the war, around 80 per cent of all food consumed in Britain was grown in Britain. As petrol was also rationed, grocers were restricted on where they could get their stock from: it had to come from the nearest producer or wholesaler. Not only that, but you had to register with your local grocer rather than looking further afield for your weekly rations. This was an incredibly effective way to cut food miles and waste in the food chain.

The "Dig for Victory" campaign inevitably created more awareness of seasonal produce: if you grow your own, you'll know when it's available. In addition, only having access to what's grown locally is always going to put a buyer in touch with when things grow.

Now

Although we're not quite back up to the bad old days of the 1930s, Britain now imports just over half of its food supply. We produce most of our meat and dairy at home these days, but less than a quarter of our fruit and veg is grown at home.

Because we're not so hot on eating local, seasonal produce, we're adding to food mileage as well. Food travels further (and we travel further to get it) so we can eat less seasonal, more processed, cheaper food. The real price of having strawberries in December goes way beyond the supermarket price tag, particularly when we're talking air freighted foods!

On the other hand, all foods now come with a country of origin label, and there's generally a Union Flag sticker on home-grown goods. But that doesn't always give the full picture about how and how far the food has been imported. By contrast, a good local farmer's market will have a policy of selling food from within a defined local area, so you can be sure you're not overburdening your environment, while fruit and veg boxes from local farms make sure your food comes from a local source.

Wednesday: time to reflect

"You learn to cook so that you don't have to be a slave to recipes. You get what's in season and you know what to do with it."[33]

Julia Child (chef, author and TV personality)

Thursday: where do I stand?

Find a space outdoors, preferably somewhere you can feel the ground beneath your feet. If you're doing this in warm weather, you could even take your shoes off.

Plant your feet. Close your eyes and breathe. Feel yourself rooted in this place, in this time.

Wherever you are, right now you are a part of this place. Breathe in and out. Notice if the air is cold or warm, if there's a breeze or if it's still. Is it quiet or is there a hum of background noise? Are there scents on the air that bring your part of the world into focus?

Acknowledge your place in this part of the world: *your* part of the world. Root yourself here; attune yourself to the seasonal comings and goings of where you are.

This is the place that nourishes you. Allow yourself to feel gratitude for this sustaining earth.

Friday: think global

Did you know that the 500 million women and men who produce 70 per cent of the world's food also make up half the world's hungry people? This is not an accident. Once again, the people who produce our food are losing out at the end of the supply chain.[34]

And once again, it's something we have the power to change.

The Fairtrade Foundation works to make us all that little bit more aware of how our purchases affect other people.[35] We can take that awareness forward to make permanent changes to our shopping habits that really support the world's smallholder farmers who supply most of our creature comforts. After all, over 4,500 products are now Fairtrade, so we should be able to find them!

And we can keep shouting about how unfair it is that seven companies control 85 per cent of tea production globally and three companies hold nearly half the global coffee production, while the growers and producers get a tiny percentage of the profits.[36]

If you're doing this challenge at the moment, then you're only able to buy food produced in the UK. But, in future, have a think about what you usually put in your shopping basket. Are you really putting your money where your mouth is?

Saturday: act local

Good news: thousands of local growers are waiting to fill up your shopping basket with tasty, seasonal produce! And there are big benefits to it:

- You'll get what's seasonal... and therefore at its best. Seasonal food is the freshest and also what your body needs right now.
- You can support the little guys. Look around for growers and producers who don't have a big outlet for their produce.
- You'll cut food miles. Environmentally, it's way better to buy local. Cut the food miles on local produce (and save them for oranges and bananas when your challenge is over!).
- You'll support your local economy. Buy local and keep your cash circulating in your area. More jobs, more prosperity... You did that with a sack of potatoes. Feels good, doesn't it?
- You'll pay a fair price. Buying from small growers can often be cheaper than over-packaged, freighted-in food because it cuts out the middle man. If it's not cheaper, it might reflect what growing food really costs.
- You'll make friends. Making friends in your community is an untold treasure. And can lead to unexpected freebies! Give local growers your support and they might remember you when they've got a surplus to shift...
- You'll protect your countryside. Buying from small and specialist producers helps them survive in a market which supports intensive food production. They're often way more in touch with the earth.

If buying local is a daunting prospect, remember: every little change helps! Could you change one or two things about your shopping habits? Even if you switched to just one local supplier for a few items on your list, you'd be helping with all of the above.

Sunday: feast

Go local: Take a seasonal walk

This is a week to get out and about in your local area – be it town, city, or countryside. Every season has its beauty so, wherever you are in the year, take some time to explore and observe.

Here are some things to look and listen out for in each season. Remember, with wildlife, "look don't touch" is always the best policy, and you should never gather berries, mushrooms, or other foods if you're not sure what you're looking for.

Spring
Buds, blossoms and spring flowers
Nests and the chirping of new little birds
Elderflowers for cordial

Summer
Returning birds, like swifts and swallows
Rapeseed in the fields
Breeze through the trees
Hot sunshine and people meeting for lunch in the park

Autumn
Big drifts of beautiful fallen leaves
Blackberries
Cobwebs covered in dew
Cold, crisp air

Winter
Frost patterns
Holly
Icy puddles, ponds, and canals
Mushrooms (take an experienced guide!)
Chestnuts
Blue heritage plaques

WEEK SIX:

Gratitude

Monday: diary entry week six

I'm into the last full week of my rations challenge. This has been a brilliant experience. There have been highs and lows.

The lows include: running out of fun things to make with potatoes, and wartime baking which is a world away from my usual eggs-and-butter extravaganza and makes for dull, flat, sawdust-y cake.

The highs include: learning to make soda bread and pastry with very few ingredients; Mary-Anne Boermans (of *The Great British Bake Off* fame) tweeting me recipe suggestions, and one dear friend lovingly photocopying every single page of her own mother's wartime scrapbook, with all the original Ministry of Food leaflets and recipes for me. Loads of vital tips on "how to make the fat ration last" and "making the most of milk". And what a privilege to see all the handwritten notes and comments from a real wartime cook!

So, when I've been ready to throw in the towel and make a tomato omelette, the generosity of people around me has reminded me of why I'm doing this and then I've given myself a mental slap and got on with it. After all, I'm not starving. I'm not wondering where my next meal will come from, or trying to eke out £1 a day for my shopping.

Meanwhile, I've formed good habits. I've developed a keener sense of what I don't need, and my shopping trolley is no longer overflowing with things I won't finish before they go off.

When you're living on rations, the main concern most days is how to manage your supply – how to make your food last the week and make the most of what you have. And I have actually really enjoyed the planning, and cooking, and making rations stretch. I find it breeds gratitude for what I have.

Gratitude seems to be the overriding emotion as the end of my challenge marches into sight. I am hugely grateful that I have had friends and family taking an interest, sharing their stories and experiences (not to mention recipes), and boosting my resolve when fadge (see the "Wartime Cookery" section for the recipe) was falling off my fork before my slightly nauseated gaze. I'm grateful for the insights into our food system that this challenge has thrown up, and the knowledge I've gained. Mostly, I'm truly grateful for the food on my plate, the choices open to me, and the fact that I live in a world of amazing abundance.

The rations regime showed true stewardship of resources. It sought not only to feed but to educate the population about food, and in doing so created a healthier nation than it had ever seen in the years before the war.

I'm starting to fantasize about my first post-rations dinner, which I'm pretty sure is going to contain eggs and some form of citrus fruit, but there are definitely some lessons I'll do my darndest to take forward:

- I definitely think local, seasonal food is the way forward. I'll be trying to live by this maxim and recognize that food from overseas is a privilege.
- I *can* live on much less than I'm used to – and buying a sensible amount cuts bills and waste. So, while I'll be looking forward to more variety post-rations, with a bit of planning, hopefully I won't increase the overall amount I buy.

If we're *all* going to have enough to eat, we should take only what we need of the world's abundance. We need food systems to work for everyone, not just people who are lucky enough to live in specific countries or have a certain access to education.

I hope the rations challenge gives you, like me, a better knowledge of how we can tread more lightly on the earth, be better stewards, better neighbours, and better humans generally. And I hope it leaves you with hope that the changes that need to be made are within our power. A little digging from all of us: just think of the victories we can claim!

Tuesday: then and now

Then

VE day (Victory in Europe day) was marked on 8 May 1945. When Hitler was finally defeated, Winston Churchill declared a public holiday. People danced and threw parties in the streets and, in London, huge crowds gathered in Whitehall and outside Buckingham Palace.

Celebrating VE Day

But the war was not entirely finished. It wasn't until August that victory was declared in Japan, and the final peace agreement wasn't signed until 2 September. I imagine those who had loved ones fighting outside Europe had to hold their breath for longer before they could finally sigh in relief that the war was ended.

Over 60 million people throughout the world were killed in the Second World War. Naturally, the celebrations when it ended were heavily tinged with sadness and loss.

Laying a wreath

Now

VE day is still commemorated every year. In 2015, on the seventieth anniversary of Victory in Europe, three days of events took place to mark the date. From services to street parties, people came together to mark the occasion and to pay their respects. Veterans joined in Armed Forces parades through

London, while the Red Arrows performed spectacular air displays overhead.

The Red Arrows

As well as a chance to celebrate over seventy years of relative peace in Europe, the anniversary offered a chance to show gratitude for all those who fought for the freedoms we now enjoy, including the food on our plates and the choices we're able to make every day – often without really thinking about it. Street parties and tea dances bring people together while remembrance services and commemorations give us time to reflect.

Although we have peace at home, our armed forces have been engaged in conflicts around the world ever since. Thinking of all that is sacrificed on our behalf and in our name, let's never stop striving, and working, and praying for peace in our world.

Wednesday: time to reflect

> *"If the only prayer you ever said was thank you, that would be enough."*

Eckhart von Hochheim
(thirteenth-century German theologian)

Thursday: where do I stand?

Excitement and joy: you are nearly at the end! If you've made it through these six weeks without cracking and frying up a plate of eggs, I salute you. I hope you're looking forward to a royal feast on Sunday.

In the midst of thinking about the celebration and abundance ahead, take time away to focus on quiet and gratitude.

Find a quiet place. Plant your feet. Breathe. This part of your journey is nearly at its destination. Take a moment to remember where you started from, and where you find yourself now. Has anything changed for you? What, if anything, did you learn? What will you give thanks for?

Broaden this out: we all stand on foundations laid by others – people whose wisdom, bravery, and sacrifice have shaped our world and the freedoms we share. In your own way and time, allow yourself to feel gratitude for the foundations they laid.

What will you build on those foundations? What will your legacy be?

Friday: think global

Spread the good news! Despite all the bad news in the world, there are reasons for hope and happiness. Here are some reasons to be cheerful: some inspiration from people determined to bring good news to their communities and the world.

- The number of undernourished people in the world has fallen by 200 million since 1990. There's still a very long way to go, but another 200 million people with enough to eat is a big leap forward.[37]

- We are reducing our food waste. France is leading the way on supermarket waste by banning supermarkets from throwing unspoiled food away.[38] Instead they have to donate it to charities and food banks. In the UK, Tesco recently scrapped "best before" dates on fruit and veg to curb unnecessary waste.[39] Frozen food chain Iceland has pledged to do away with all plastic wrap and palm oil – which is responsible for destruction of the rainforest – from all of its own-brand products.[40]

- Food waste and food poverty are big problems in the UK. But in 2018 the charity FareShare, which redistributes edible food that would otherwise go to waste, helped feed 750,000 people a week.[41]

- The British Hen Welfare Trust has rehomed more than 600,000 battery hens to date. These once battered and unloved birds are now happily rehomed with families across Britain. Happy hens, happy eggs, happy families![42]

- In 2018, the Peace Pledge Union (PPU), which sells white poppies for Remembrance Day, had a record year. White poppies first appeared in 1933 and are a symbol of peace and remembrance of all victims of war. One hundred years on from Armistice Day, more and more people are making a stand for peace in our world and rejecting the waste and violence war inevitably brings.[43]

- A year after the murder of politician Jo Cox, hundreds of thousands of people took part in The Great Get-Together – a nationwide celebration of communities inspired by her belief that "We are far more united and have far more in common than that which divides us." In 2018, 300,000 people took part in 45,000 events across the UK. And there are already 121,988 get-togethers planned for 2019.[44]
- Economics Student, Joy Youwakim, is researching how to grow food on top of disused landfill sites in Southeast Austin, Texas. So far, she's grown radishes, lettuces, peppers, aubergines and cucumbers to name a few. So far, tests on the food she's growing look good – the food is testing safe to eat. If Joy's method works, that could mean hundreds of thousands – if not millions – of acres of disused wasteland turned into food for hungry people.[45]

Saturday: act local

Hopefully, the rations journey has been a useful experience, one that has put you in touch with your community and the world around you. So instead of action suggestions today, maybe now is the time to think about how life will be going forward.

Maybe you'll make some new friends on your local high street or market.

Maybe you'll be more open to chatting to your neighbours and people who live nearby.

Maybe, when you do your supermarket shop, you'll find wonder in small things we take for granted... the marvel of international cooperation that brings oranges and coffee to our door.

Maybe you'll join a Great Get-Together this summer, lobby your MP on issues that matter, or sign a petition to change some of the injustices in the world.

If nothing else, maybe you'll be able to free up space in your day-to-day routine just to breathe, to feel connected to our world and give thanks for its abundance.

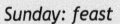

Sunday: feast

You did it! Time to celebrate!

Gather your friends and family. If anyone has been particularly supportive or helpful during your challenge, they should definitely be around to help you celebrate now.

Although you might have had enough of rations by now and technically you have finished, you'll find wartime party food ideas in the "Wartime Cookery" section of this book, as well as more exciting ways to "update your plate" using seasonal food.

Here are some ideas for your Victory Feast:

Good weather

If it's appropriate you could organize a party in your street and invite the neighbours, in true VE day spirit. Find some Vera Lynn music to play and celebrate.

On a smaller scale, why not throw a garden party? Set up some informal chairs and tables, move your speakers outside and invite everyone in for some ginger beer and oranges. Organize some games for any small people – treasure hunts always go down well in garden settings.

Bad weather

Don't let bad weather ruin the fun! Why not set up a 1940s' home cinema? Use a large sheet or blank wall and a projector and play old movies for the afternoon. Serve ginger beer and home-made lemonade.

Or... go the whole hog and throw a VE party! Insist on 1940s' get-up: wiggle dresses and uniforms, serve sidecars and damson gin and don't forget to break out the bunting!

LIVING ON RATIONS:

Other People's Accounts

Jim and Patricia Wilkinson lived in Britain during the Second World War. They shared their experiences of living on rations with me.

Patricia

I was seven when the war started. I had already been evacuated from London to a farm in Somerset which belonged to family friends, Aunt Audrey and Uncle Charlie. It was quite a contrast: we were a mile and a half from the nearest village and seven miles from the nearest town. Aunt Audrey looked after me and four other evacuee children at one time. We heard the siren once during the war; we were up the top of Exmoor. In the distance we heard this funny wailing sound and were told it was the siren.

My father and mother were both in the National Fire Service and my father was in the overseas division. I didn't know what that meant. In the year of D-Day, I was in floods of tears because I thought my father had gone over to Normandy and I was worried he was going to be killed. He didn't actually go overseas – he was in London the whole time, which wasn't much safer, but I wasn't to know that.

Aunt Audrey was very artistic. The end of the house was white which stuck out like a sore thumb and she was told to do something about it because it was visible from the air. She painted a wonderful mural over the side of the house with huntsmen on it. It blended right in but it was a work of art as well.

We didn't have vegetable plots as such, but we did have chickens; both the eggs and the chickens were an important part of our diet – the chickens added to the meat ration. We had rabbits too.

They had a little terrier called Danny. One day we came home from school to find a very woebegone Danny tied up in the kitchen with a chicken covered in mustard hanging round his neck. He'd got into the chicken run, pinched this chicken and upset all the others, so he'd been there all day with this mustard-covered chicken which he couldn't eat because it burned his mouth! We thought Aunt Audrey was terribly cruel but Danny never went near the chickens again!

I don't really have much memory of wartime rationing; Aunt Audrey would have handled the rations books and, at seven, you just eat what you're given. I remember having dried eggs though. They were nasty!

Sweets affected me of course. I've always liked sweets, and I still do. Maybe that's because we were rationed. We gave up sugar in our tea so Aunt Audrey could use the sugar ration for cakes.

I remember the milk in the dairy being organized to send away for rations, but Aunt Audrey would also make Somerset cream. She used to say, 'Don't tell anybody, we're not supposed to!' I'm not sure but the cream might have gone to people in the village.

The other day, my granddaughter saw me putting butter in the butter dish and I automatically scraped the remains of it off the wrapper before I threw it away. She said: "What did you do that for Grandma?" It's a hangover from the war; you don't waste.

It's horrendous what gets wasted now. If I could pass anything to the next generation it would be: "Don't waste it, use it."

Jim

I was six at the start of the war. I remember I was half-listening to the radio, when my father said: "Hmmm! War's been declared then." I didn't understand what it meant. Why should I at that age? It didn't mean much.

We lived off the main road between Hounslow and London. My mother's parents lived on the main road and my Uncle Alf lived the other side, so our gardens converged. Although you weren't supposed to, we made gates in the fences so it was like one big communal garden.

Grandma and Granddad kept chickens and rabbits, we kept rabbits, and Uncle Alf kept ducks. The back garden was divided into three: the first third was lawn and flowers. Then there were roses growing up to separate it from the vegetable plot, then at the bottom were fruit trees. We grew everything: sweetcorn, cabbages – you name it, Dad grew it.

I remember helping Dad to kill Uncle Alf's ducks. There was no shielding us from that sort of thing – it was food and we weren't sentimental about it. If you wanted meat you had to kill an animal. I was quite used to it.

There was always fish near us, but you didn't get to choose what fish you had, you just had what was there.

We had loads of fruit. I remember jam and marmalade making, though don't ask me where we got the oranges!

I went to a friend's house once and, as we were sitting there, we heard an enormous bang. My friend said: 'Something's blown up!' but his mum said: 'Oh no! It's the tomatoes!' She had all these tomatoes she'd been bottling up and they started exploding one by one! The official accounts always make everything sound so efficient, but I'm pretty sure there were lots of incidents like the exploding tomatoes.

Where I lived was a main thoroughfare into London. Not only did we have the big air raid shelters but also anti-aircraft guns. Two doors up from us was a gas main, which was incendiary bombed. My father worked in a factory which narrowly missed being bombed in one raid.

People did muck in and help each other. There was a widowed lady with a daughter, and another family a few doors down, who needed help. The men all got together and built them air raid shelters in the garden. I don't think anyone in our area was hard up for food; almost everyone had their own chickens or rabbits. We didn't need to share it about so much, but when there was a need, people helped.

I think the current generation would benefit from living through the war. You lived healthily, because the bad stuff wasn't around.

You cooked properly and ate decently. People now are very fussy, but if you just have what's there, you waste less and eat better.

Everything I put into my black bin, I hate. I don't want to put things in there. We have a broken shopping trolley with a plastic lined bag. I don't want to throw it out because it won't decompose. I'll probably use it for putting garden rubbish in or turn it into a birdseed bag.

Our landfill rubbish, which is collected once a fortnight, consists of a very small amount. The sack is more than the rubbish inside it.

Living on rations definitely made an impression on our lives. Every scrap of food has to be used. Just yesterday we got upset throwing away a tiny bit of mashed potato. It sounds ridiculous but living through the war teaches you not to waste. There are always people worse off than you.

Andrew de la Haye and Yolande Watson run a vegan smallholding, and self-sufficiency holidays from their eco-friendly home in Herefordshire.

Yolande

We wanted to find a way to live that nurtured ourselves and others: we wanted to tread lightly on the earth. Now we live on what we grow and our household is more or less carbon-neutral. We live on around £5,000 a year. We heat our house with only solar energy and wood burning. I even make my own toiletries.

We trade our skills and services through the Local Exchange and Trade Scheme, or barter with our local community: for example, we look after our neighbour's dogs and they "pay" us in wood, or we pick all the fruit off the trees for our elderly neighbours and share the bounty. We forage all the time. (I like to think we are the human "Borrowers"!)

If we need something, we always try to make it ourselves first. For instance, we've laid our own hedges and made our own drystone wall. We've made a lot of our furniture out of free pallets and materials we've collected. Since we are known as the "eco-couple", our neighbours and friends also ask if we need something before they throw it out or give it away. I buy my clothes from the charity shops and know where to go to buy tops for £1. Last Tuesday, I bought three tops and a pair of shorts for £2!

We do own our own home and not having a mortgage has made a huge difference to how much we need to live on.

Our way of life is a philosophy of "having enough". So many people want more, but more means "more stuff, more insurance, more worries..."

And, there are many who've moved to the countryside but don't engage or get involved in their community. Living in a community is part of treading lightly on the earth. It's about recognizing and nurturing the biodiversity and synergy of life. We cannot live in isolation; humans need to help and connect with each other to create sustainable options.

Andrew

We met when we were both on a voyage of discovery about the world, ecology and ourselves. We came to the realization that the way society operates leaves us out of touch with the earth and our own bodies.

We're passionate about eating seasonally. The earth provides what you need when the body needs it. For instance, in winter, when it's so much colder, you tend to get more root vegetables, providing starch and warmth. We grow a huge variety of produce on our smallholding – we try to grow our proteins and starches so we can use them all year round. We try to grow enough so that we have enough for every day. We don't freeze much food at all – we prefer to eat things when they're fresh – but we do bottle and preserve fruits and make our own jams, pickles and drinks. We also make our own bread.

The idea is we don't grow everything, but we are self-sufficient. We're part of the Dean Forest Food Hub, which was a finalist in the 2016 BBC Food and Farming Awards. It's a local organization which links up various producers around the forest and enables them to sell their excess. The Hub passes on food to customers. A shopping list goes up on Tuesdays, so we decide what our weekly surplus is and put it on the website. On Fridays, we have a frantic morning picking and packing our surplus and taking it to a local farm, where they make up customers' boxes and deliver them in the afternoon. We pick the courgettes in the morning and the customer can eat them in the afternoon. It's competitive, local, low in food miles and so fresh. Supermarkets just can't do that. We sell excess produce through the Hub and use that account to buy produce we aren't growing at the moment, like organic oats, coffee, etc.

To me the smallholding is one big playground.

The way we grow is completely organic. I started out doing crop rotation, with four beds – for roots, alliums, legumes, and brassicas.

Originally, I'd rotate the planting every year. We don't do that any more; I don't like digging – it's hard work! What we do is put lots of horse manure on over the winter and, by the spring, it's been broken down. The living things in the soil break down the nutrients, and create the water channels the plants need. It's a symbiotic relationship between the plant and the living soil.

The other thing I'm moving away from is regimented rows. When you grow one type of crop all together, you have to keep moving them as they get diseases: the pests know exactly where to find them. If you spread them out and diversify, they don't get diseases as the pests can't find them so easily.

We're studying permaculture, biodynamic farming, organic farming, but we're doing it by working with nature, finding these ideas and trying them. We read about ideas and try them, and we learn that way; we experience things first hand. For instance, the Native Americans grow corn, beans and squash together. The way it works is that the corn is a pole for the beans and the beans bring nitrogen into the soil. So, the corn supports the bean and gets fed by the bean. The squash provides ground cover and stops weeds from growing. The beans are our source of protein for the winter; nature dries them out and we store them.

I'm a bit of a student of compost heaps! The composting technique we use is a Second World War method, created and pioneered by Maye E. Bruce. Miss Bruce experimented with flower essences, oak bark, and honey, and came up with her own biodynamic method of composting. This is the method we use and it makes wonderful organic compost in eight weeks.

The formula was used in the war from a book written in 1940 and it's failsafe. It's nettle and yarrow, dried and ground into a powder. Then you add camomile, oak bark, dandelion, honey, and valerian. And it works.

When we went on a big trip around the world in 2012, we decided that the less we spent, the more fun we'd have. We'd stay in the cheapest hostels and walk everywhere. And it was amazing; we saw and learned so much.

I think things are too cheap these days, too easily available. How can this be? It doesn't feel right to us that things which are seasonal are available all year round. If you keep things local, you keep things seasonal and in balance. It's better for the earth and for ourselves.

I understand that not everyone can do what we've done; we own our own home and we can choose to live this way. Not living this way doesn't make anyone bad. What I hope is that we can provide a model. A few years ago, I realized that you don't need to change the world. It's an enormous world and that is a very daunting prospect.

But, if you can make some changes in your corner of the planet, then great. The aim, as we see it, is just to move the world by an inch.

Peggy Wheatley was sixteen when war broke out. She joined the Women's Land Army and spent the war years between Wokingham and London.

Peggy

When the war started, I was working for my aunt who ran a sub-post office in Chiswick. She rang up and said, "Tell Peggy not to come back 'til the war's over!" I stayed home for a while but, in the end, I said to Mum, "I can't stay at home, we don't know when the war's going to finish!" So I went back to work.

I joined the Land Army at seventeen. I wanted to join the Wrens but then I found Mum crying in the kitchen because she was worried about me; she already had three sons in the forces. I said, "All right, I'll go in the Land Army instead."

My farm was in Wokingham near Reading. At seventeen, I was the baby, not that I got any special treatment! One time they ploughed up a field that had never been used before, and we worked on a Saturday which was our time off. We got thruppence an hour and we had to plant the whole field.

I decided one day that we should ask the farmer for more money. We all marched up to him but, when he asked what we wanted, nobody spoke! I thought some of the older ones would say something and they didn't say a word. So eventually I spoke up. We didn't get anywhere though; the pay stayed at thruppence an hour.

I stayed for about three years, but then I got rheumatism in the head and couldn't go back. The rheumatism was caused by working in the rain; we got soaked to the skin. They just couldn't find a raincoat that stopped the rain, nothing stopped it. The farmer's lads used to shelter in the sheds and watch us work in it! I still suffer with my joints and veins from my days in the Land Army because it was such hard work. We started at 6 a.m. in the morning in summer, and finished at 4 p.m.

In the winter, we collected cabbages covered in ice; you had to chip the ice away before you could get at them. We dug potatoes; you had to kneel on the ground and drop them in a bucket you held between your knees. There were two conscientious objectors who took the produce to market every morning at 5 a.m. by horse and cart. They worked very hard, until 10 p.m. at night.

We had great entertainment. I used to work with my rollers in so I could go out afterwards. I lived next door to the pub and we played darts with the squaddies in the evenings: the Army, the Air Force and the Canadian troops were stationed nearby. We used to go to dances in a nearby village, get home at 4 a.m. and be up at 6 a.m. to go to work! On those days, we'd be in bed by 6 p.m. as we were all exhausted.

There was only one bomb in Reading. The girls from Reading used to say, "It can't be that bad in London." Those of us from London didn't argue; we'd been through it and that was that. That one bomb came as a shock to them.

It was hard work, but it was a lovely life. If you lived in the country, you did do better for food. We had plenty of eggs at that time. When I got married after the war, we didn't have eggs any more, just egg powder. When real eggs came in, we didn't know how to use them, I had got so used to cooking with egg powder!

After the Land Army, I worked as a cashier in a butcher's on Baker Street. I dealt with people's rations. There was usually beef and lamb, but not chicken – that was a real treat. We'd put a notice up when we'd got rabbit or offal. It wasn't rationed but you had to mark the book to make sure it was shared out properly.

It was up to you what you did with your rations – if you went for the less expensive cuts you got more for your rations. People often lived on vegetables and potatoes in the week and had meat at the weekends.

There was a black market but you needed money for that sort of thing. My mum was a milk lady with a horse and cart and my dad worked incredibly hard as a removal man. He did bring home money, but we weren't well off. We lived in flats for poor people in Fulham. Dad was in the Home Guard as well; he'd work all day and be Home Guard at night.

I didn't find rations boring but then Mum was a good cook. We had shrimps and winkles as fish wasn't rationed. We ate seasonally as well, which was good – I wish that would come back. We were rationed and poor, but we counted ourselves better than most.

We didn't really have birthday parties, but Christmas was always nice. You had to save up your coupons for it, but you could get a good piece of beef. My mum made everything – all the stuffing and puddings.

I see children now with fizzy drinks and treats. We didn't have that. We couldn't afford it anyway, even after the war. I don't think it's good for you. That kind of food was for birthdays and holidays.

If your kids were evacuated, it was hard to get to see them. You had to work, nobody had cars. But when the kids weren't evacuated, that could be difficult too. My mum-in-law could make a meal out of a potato, but she'd often give the food to her kids and go without herself.

Every family had losses, and when people came back from the war, they didn't have any help, practical or emotional. They were a tough generation. People did their bit and we looked after each other.

We definitely celebrated VE day. I meant to go to Trafalgar Square, but I never got there because I got drunk! I kept meeting customers on the way who were buying me drinks. It was the worst thing I ever did in my life – I missed Trafalgar Square and was ill for a week. I never got drunk again!

Women ran the country during the war: munitions factories, running the buses, and so on. When the men came back a lot of women stepped aside so the men could have their jobs back. We respected that they'd gone to fight. But I carried on at the butcher's; I did their holiday relief and travelled all over London to fill in.

If we saved now as we did during the war, we'd be a very rich country. We never wasted anything and I still live like that. I'm careful with water, because we didn't have running hot water for a long time either. There was no waste.

I don't remember the end of rationing; it happened so slowly. My favourite joke: two boys were coming home on the train from being evacuated and an old lady offered them a banana. They'd never seen one before and started to eat it. All of a sudden, the train went through a tunnel and the one boy said to the other: "Charlie, don't eat that, it sends you blind!"

What would I pass on to the next generation? Well, I'd say "Don't have regrets. The world doesn't owe you a living. The grass isn't greener on the other side of the fence. Stop and watch the flowers along the way. Do to others as you would have them do unto you." Those are the sayings I try to live by.

Elaine Mendoza and her husband Colin Wavell left London in the 1970s to live self-sufficiently. When I started my rations challenge, Elaine lovingly photocopied her mother's wartime cookbook for me.

Elaine

I met Colin in my late twenties, when I was studying and he was a lecturer in an art school. I'd never left London for more than six weeks, but Colin grew up in a village. His granny kept chickens and grew vegetables, and he had fond memories of that time.

We were sitting on a bridge in Somerset on holiday, when we discovered we shared a dream about leaving London. We read John Seymour's book *Practical Self-Sufficiency*, which started the whole "good life" movement in the 1970s, and thought "if he can do it, so can we!"

So we spent the drought of 1976 driving long distances in a car which kept overheating, investigating ways to make the dream a reality. We had no luck, but when I went back to university, a friend mentioned a woman who'd just bought a house in Somerset with some land and outbuildings, who needed help developing its use.

That got us started. We lived there for a couple of years and we did everything we set out to do.

We wanted to lead a life that was less about owning lots of stuff, and more about a direct relationship with our food and more in rhythm with the seasons. We lived in a flat within the house, which was basically a couple of rooms. There was no plumbing in the kitchen: we had a sink with a bucket under it!

Colin had gardening and manual skills, while I was the organizer. We had grown some vegetables and kept chickens in London, but we learned the rest on the go. Fortunately, we made friends among local smallholders who gave us advice and encouragement, and we attended courses at the local Technical College, and Soil Association talks.

We soon bought goats to give us dairy produce and the manure helped grow the vegetables. It was a whole system: we grew fodder for the goats and I started dairying. I made soft and hard goats' cheese, but I was chucking whey down the drain which you're not supposed to do as it's highly acidic. It's also a terrible waste. Then we realized that what you do with whey is feed pigs! We bought three – reared two for meat and kept one as a sow. I haven't eaten pork since we stopped rearing our own; what you get in the shops is unrecognizable compared with what we used to produce. We also added bees and more chickens, hatching eggs and rearing chicks. We sold on laying hens and ate the cockerels.

We ploughed all the money we made back into the smallholding. Our part-time jobs covered rent and bills, but we tended not to eat much that we didn't grow. We sold surplus produce and we used to take this big jar of coins to the feed mill for supplies. We must have looked crazy!

After a couple of years, we needed to look for a new venture. I found an advert in the *Soil Association Magazine*: an estate in Dorset needed a gardener and a cook/cleaner, so off we went.

The thirteen-acre estate had a huge Soil Association-rated vegetable garden with a crinkle-crankle wall which had been built by Napoleonic prisoners. Part of the garden was used to raise seed for a seed library of rare vegetable varieties. It was just the most beautiful place. *[See www.deanscourt.org/the-garden]*

We lived in a cottage on the estate. Colin did the garden and I cooked and cleaned for the house. I also ran a wholefood tea room in the summer. It was fascinating looking after such an interesting place with its wood panelling and stained glass.

I loved cooking in the family's massive kitchen, although they did have a completely out-of-control dog who got into the larder once and ate all the cakes for the tea room! They also had peacocks, which are beautiful, but terrible for vegetable gardens. Colin was trying to grow rare vegetables and the peacocks kept flying in and scratching everything up. They terrorized Cyril, our cockerel, as well!

In the end we had to stop. We earned very little and had no prospects there. I was pregnant, and my stepson stayed with us regularly, so we realized we needed something with a bit more future. We sold everything except the bees and the chickens. Selling the sow was a blow; pigs are clever and sociable, and Colin used to love going to the sty to chat to her. And I still miss my goats.

Then some friends told us about a health food shop for sale in Somerset and we thought, 'We could run that!' We took on the shop on the 1st of April which was perhaps an auspicious date! My dad had a small house in the area where we were able to live. It was a lovely place to have a baby, with beautiful views across the valley, and running a shop allowed us to share childcare.

Sadly, although we improved the business, we couldn't build it as an asset and generate enough capital for a place of our own with land. People were becoming aware about additives in food, and the supermarkets caught on very quickly. Suddenly everything was additive-free, and we couldn't compete with the big chains' prices. We did raise a mortgage for a house of our own, so we achieved some security, though not our own smallholding.

Life since the shop has gone off on many tangents. We've done everything from painting and decorating, to adult education and parenting classes. I even worked in a department store café one Christmas.

We always ate well though. I remember my daughter, Nancy, being a bit nonplussed the first time I gave her pocket money and said, 'That's yours to do what you like with; if you want to buy sweets, that's your choice.' I think it took about six weeks for her to realize I really wasn't going to tell her off if she bought unhealthy treats!

A lot of how we've chosen to live comes from what we inherited from our family and the war generation. We both came from families who didn't waste. When we were smallholding, we'd use the whole animal. I used to make brawn and sausages, even what I'd call an apology for bacon; it didn't look good, but it tasted fine! I still make chutneys and jam, it's much nicer to make it yourself.

My family was relatively comfortable, but my dad was a self-employed film-maker: his attitude was that once he'd finished a film, he was out of work and he made decisions on that basis. So, we had to be careful with money. We didn't have a car until I was fourteen.

My grandmother was an amazing cook. She used to cater for weddings and made all kinds of incredible pastries. We loved visiting Grandma because there'd be meringues and cheesecake for tea! My mother was certainly not a plain cook; that pride in your cooking definitely got handed down.

One time, Grandma visited, and I was preparing a meal. She sat and watched me and afterwards she said, "That was amazing – it was like watching myself." It was the nicest compliment she could have given me. I have her secret recipes – she gave them to my mum, and I've given them to Nancy. They're an inheritance. Some are written on the back of old envelopes which is how she recorded things – and some are very idiosyncratic: she'll say you need a "walnut of butter" or a "moderate oven" but you sort of know what she means!

Mum was sixteen when the war broke out and, two years later, she joined the Wrens. She met my dad in Portsmouth where they were both stationed and she was married by twenty-one. She had my brother a year later. She probably hadn't done a lot of housekeeping – I don't know how she managed, to be honest. But she was a very capable woman, and I have her wartime recipe book. I remember it from my childhood, and Dad gave it to me when he moved from the family home.

The book is an old notebook of Dad's; you can just about read his name and "1942 Torpedo course" on the front. Mum recycled it because, of course, in wartime you didn't buy a new notebook for your recipes. It's full of cuttings and leaflets that she stuck in. She indexed it all as well. I love that she stuck pudding recipes over Dad's torpedo notes. There's so much of both of them in here; probably an engineer would be as interested in it as a cook!

Mum used the book well into the 1950s, adding lots of more interesting recipes than the Ministry of Food leaflets provided. There's a recipe for a Genoese sponge which I'm pretty sure she never made, but a lot of chocolate recipes I know she used; we were all chocolate fiends!

Wartime rations were so spartan. The National Loaf sounds awful! The food we produced wasn't spartan at all; it was healthy, wholesome and tasted wonderful.

Since we've retired, Colin has gone back to growing and we have an allotment. So, we once more have the satisfaction of a home-grown table. We buy meat from a local butcher and I tend to shop on the high street for everything else except groceries; we like being rooted in our community.

We shop in the supermarket from a basic list which can seem a bit boring but stops you buying things you don't need. We still have the same relationship to food, even if we don't produce so much ourselves these days. It needs to be simple, unmessed-around-with but creatively cooked. Where possible we like to know its origins too. We waste very little, which these days is more of an ethic than a necessity. That was what the smallholding was about for us. Our motivation for running the shop was the same but included providing good food for other people too. We still wanted to live by ethical standards; we never overcharged for anything and we treated our employees decently.

Our upbringing enabled us to live on very little. Nancy is the same; she can spend money when she has it, but she's absolutely fine not to. At lean times, it helps you cope better.

I don't regret anything; it's been an amazing experience. You have to use your imagination to live that way, and not be too proud. You need a 'can-do' attitude.

We've never fitted any kind of mould, but we enjoyed it. The food was amazing, it was a good way to live, and we were good role models. For us, the personal is political, and one way to make a contribution is how you live your own life."

Wartime Cookery

Wartime cookery

This is less a recipe section than a guide to cooking on rations. As Julia Child said, you learn to cook so that you don't have to be a slave to recipes.

There's a wealth of useful tips and tricks in the Ministry of Food leaflets and I have, of course, drawn heavily on them. But, unsurprisingly, many of the recipes themselves are now dated and I didn't find them too appetizing. Many of the original wartime recipes deliberately lent themselves to a bit of improvisation, because they're based on the understanding that you may not have all the ingredients needed at any given time. So, while I've included a few recipes from the Ministry of Food which have made their way into my everyday cooking repertoire, much of this section is advice to help you eat well on rations, while still allowing space for invention.

There are a number of marvellous modern inventions that wouldn't have been available to the wartime cook: fridges, stick blenders and non-stick pans, all of which help the savvy modern cook save time, waste and, importantly, fat ration. I would advocate using these – although, again, it is up to you how strict you want to be, what you want to gain from this and how you want your challenge to look. It is perfectly possible to follow the 1940s ration to the letter while allowing for the fact that British cooking and kitchen equipment has come a long way.

For me, I'd rather this book motivated you to live well on less and local than made you so fed up with potatoes and heavy pastry that you could weep. So, I've included four lovely seasonal dinner menus to enjoy with family and friends at the end of this section: delicious, inspiring meals I created with my good friend and chef Ian Barnes, who is passionate about local, seasonal fresh food. While these recipes are "rations-compliant", I'd feed them to anyone, on any occasion.

All recipes are for four people, unless otherwise stated.

Top tips to stretch your rations

A lot of these tips are straight from the Ministry of Food. Others are useful things I've noticed along the way.

- Use your fat ration sparingly. It's so useful for making pie crusts and baking, it's a shame to waste it on frying. If you can poach, steam, or boil, do that instead. You can drain your frying pan dripping into a cup and save it in the fridge.
- Make stock from your chicken carcass by boiling it up in a pan of cold water with some herbs and seasoning, and a carrot or two if you have them. Simmer for about four hours until it is a clear amber colour. Skim the top as necessary. Pass it through a sieve to remove the bits and bones. Allow to cool for an hour and then divide into useful portions and refrigerate or freeze. It will keep for about three days in the fridge or a few months in the freezer.
- These days we have the advantage of non-stick pans. I use them as they cut the need for grease or fat.
- Don't be a slave to the recipes! Look for seasonal and store cupboard alternatives; most wartime recipes lend themselves to this.
- A lot of wartime recipes list dried herbs and spices, including curry powder, as flavourings for meals. The chances are that spices wouldn't have been much in the shops during the war years but most households would have had them from before rationing began. My take is: if you had them in the cupboard at the start of your challenge, it's not cheating to use them up, but avoid buying new ones.

- I am not a fan of wartime pastry. I can't see that it's as nice as a lovely mashed potato topping on your casserole, which also saves you flour and fat. But there are pastry recipes, should you be longing for a pie, and I've added a shortcrust pastry recipe in case it comes in handy. To be truly wartime, bear in mind that most flour was wholemeal and, therefore, much heavier than white.
- I'd suggest using the cheese ration in separate meals from the meat ration. Wartime cooks were encouraged to make vegetarian meals during the week to eke out the meat ration, and cheese is such a wonder food it does deserve its own slot in your weekly menu. Use it in pies and on top of bakes, etc., sprinkled over salads, in sandwiches and pasties.

Breakfasts

> "A good breakfast every day is the first rule in the book of good health."
>
> **War Cookery Leaflet Number 15**

Fadge (Irish potato cakes)

225 g (8 oz) mashed potato
0.5 tsp salt
25–50 g (1–2 oz) flour

Method

Mix potato, salt and enough flour to make a stiff dough. Roll out about half a centimetre (quarter of an inch) thick and cut into eight wedges. Fry in a greased pan until browned on both sides. Serve with bacon if you have it.

◇◇◇

Porridge (for one)

Half a cup of rolled porridge oats
240–340 ml (8–12 fl oz) water
Dash of milk and a sprinkle of sugar (optional)

Method

Mix the rolled porridge oats with the water. Either boil on the hob or in the microwave for a couple of minutes. Add a dash of milk and a sprinkle of sugar if you like.

Eggy in the basket (for one)

1 fresh or reconstituted egg
2 slices bread (stale is fine)
Salt and pepper
Dripping or oil

Method

Beat the egg. Cut holes from the centre of each slice of bread with small scone cutter – don't do away with the extra circles of bread. Dip the bread slices quickly into water and fry in a greased pan on one side until golden brown. Turn on to the other side, pour half the egg into the hole in each slice of bread, and cook until the bread is nicely browned and the egg is cooked through. You can fry the circles in the same way and replace them on the tops of your slices.

◇◇◇

Swiss breakfast dish (uncannily like muesli!)[46]

225 g (8 oz) rolled oats
8 tbsp milk
2–3 tbsp raisins/other dry fruit or 4–5 tbsp cooked rhubarb/
  other fresh fruit
2 tbsp sugar (if you like)

Method

Soak the oats overnight in just enough water to cover. In the morning, mix in all the other ingredients then serve.

Milk

Salads for all seasons

Salads are so versatile and easy, you probably don't need much instruction! As a general rule, you grab handfuls of seasonal salad and veg, wash it, then chop, grate, or rip it, and dash it about in a bowl with a splash of vinaigrette. Use the seasonal calendar at the end of the book and, if you're unsure, here are some handy tips from the Ministry of Food and me!

> *"There is hardly a root or green vegetable that does not deserve a place in a salad."*
> **War Cookery Leaflet Number 5**

- Put at least one green leafy vegetable in every salad. Don't forget this would include raw cabbage, spinach, sprouts, kale and watercress. You're not limited to lettuce.
- Add root vegetables such as raw or cooked beetroot, carrot, swede, parsnip (grated or in small cubes), or cooked potatoes.
- The more colour and flavour you add the better. Radishes, onions, peas and beans, chicory, celery, cucumber, tomatoes, and red cabbage all add flavour and texture. These days, a wide variety of chillies are grown locally (or you can even grow your own on the windowsill) if you like your salad with a kick, although they weren't widely available in the war years.
- Fruit is also lovely in salads; shredded or finely sliced apple, strawberries or raspberries – even a few raisins or sultanas tossed in – add interest. Just add fruit as close to eating/serving as possible; apple especially goes brown quickly.
- If you toss salad well, you don't need much dressing at all.

I use 1 tbsp oil, 1 tbsp vinegar and a little dab of mustard, shaken up or stirred vigorously. Toss everything very thoroughly in a bowl until the whole salad is lightly coated. If you're short on oil, just use a little vinegar to moisten it and season well.

Soups

Soup is fantastic. It's a massive shot of vitamins in a bowl, and is just so easy and cheap to make. My better half, who is renowned for his brilliant veggie soups, never pre-fries the onions or adds oil to his soups and they taste amazing. Good news for your fat ration! Great soup is all in the combinations. Just boil everything with some stock until it's cooked through and soft. In these days of kitchen gadgetry, I won't apologize for advocating a stick blender, but if you're a wartime purist or don't have one, these ideas would work well with everything diced up small and cooked as a broth. Here are our favourite seasonal combinations – each recipe serves four.

◇◇◇

Spring: Minty leek and potato soup

1 kg (2 lb 8 oz) new potatoes
3 leeks
About a litre (1.75 pints) of stock (or enough to cover comfortably)
A little oil or butter
A couple of good handfuls of fresh mint, plus extra for garnish
Salt and pepper

Method

Scrub and dice the potatoes and boil with two roughly chopped leeks in the stock (making sure there is enough stock to cover vegetables comfortably). Meanwhile, finely slice a third leek and gently fry in a little oil or butter for about 5 minutes until soft and buttery but not too browned. Set this aside for a garnish. When the potatoes are thoroughly cooked, add a couple of good handfuls of fresh mint to the soup and whizz with a stick blender. Divide into bowls and sprinkle the fried leeks over the top. Chop a little extra mint over the leeks and season to taste.

◇◇◇

Summer: "Sunny" soup

4 corn-on-the-cobs
2 onions
4 red and yellow peppers
Small chilli
About 1 litre (1.75 pints) stock
Salt and pepper

Method

Place the corn-on-the-cobs in a pan of water and boil for about 5 minutes or until tender. Use a sharp knife to scrape all the corn off the cobs. Roughly chop the onions, red and yellow peppers, and a small chilli (to taste) and add them to a pan with the sweetcorn. Boil everything up in the stock until everything is tender. Whizz with a stick blender and season to taste.

◇◇◇

Autumn: Squashed pumpkin soup

1 butternut squash
1 smallish pumpkin
About 1 litre (1.75 pints) stock
1 onion
2 cloves of garlic
1 cup orange lentils, thoroughly rinsed (optional)
Some fresh or dried thyme
Salt and pepper

Method

Peel, deseed and chop the butternut squash and pumpkin. Pop
in a pan with the stock, onion, cloves of garlic and rinsed lentils
(optional). Boil it up, add some fresh or dried thyme. Blend and
season to taste.

◇◇

Winter: Winter wonder soup

1 onion
1 swede
4 parsnips
About 1 litre (1.75 pints) stock
1 punnet of mushrooms (any sort)
About 250 g (9 oz) cooked and shelled chestnuts
A little nutmeg (optional)
Salt and pepper

Method

Peel and chop the onion, swede, and parsnips. Add to a pan with
the stock, a generous punnet of cleaned mushrooms (any sort)
and the cooked and shelled chestnuts. Boil until everything is
nice and soft, then whizz with the stick blender, adding seasoning
and a little nutmeg if you have it in the store cupboard.

Making the most of cheese

On a rationed diet, cheese is such a valuable food and the thing I found most difficult to stretch. I would really advocate not using it in the same dish as your meat ration, but on its own as a vegetarian main. Homity pie (recipe below) was one meal I'd make over and over, wartime or not. Meanwhile, here are some more tips.

> "Cheese is an A1 food, better than meat for building firm muscles. It builds strong bones and teeth too."
>
> War Cookery Leaflet Number 12

- Grating cheese makes it go further.
- If you use it with sandwiches, mix grated cheese with parsley, spring onions, and pickles so you need less cheese.
- Add it to salads to make them into a meal.
- Many wartime families nominated one family member to be vegetarian so they could get a bigger cheese ration. You might fancy following suit if you're doing this challenge as a family or group.

Homity pie

Shortcrust pastry (see recipe in "Wartime pastry and bread" later in this section)
4 large potatoes, scrubbed and chopped into small cubes
2 large leeks, scrubbed and chopped into small cubes
1 cored eating apple, scrubbed and chopped into small cubes
2 cloves garlic, chopped
1 egg
Butter or margarine
100–175 g (4–6 oz) cheese
Fresh or dried thyme
Salt and pepper

Method

Roll the pastry out into a 25 x 15 cm greased pie dish and place it into oven on 200°C for about 10 minutes or so to half cook. Boil the potatoes until tender, then drain and set aside. Chop the leeks and garlic and sauté gently with a bit of butter or margarine until cooked. Add plenty of thyme and the chopped apple and toss together. Add the potatoes to the leeks, with the whisked egg, a little more butter or margarine, 50 g (2 oz) of the grated cheese, and seasoning. Stir. Spread the mixture evenly on top of the half-baked pastry, then top with the remaining cheese, a sprinkle of extra thyme, and pepper. Cook in oven at 220°C until the top is browned. Remove and leave to cool a bit before serving.

◇◇

Making potatoes interesting

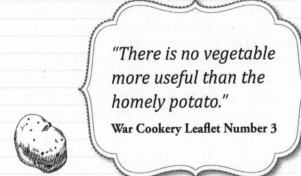

> *"There is no vegetable more useful than the homely potato."*
>
> **War Cookery Leaflet Number 3**

No two ways about it: you eat a *lot* of spuds on rations. Home-grown and plentiful, they replaced imported wheat and were used in every possible role, from plain boiled to pie crust. As such, it's tricky not to get bored with them. But there are some recipes I wouldn't have done without. Here are some ways to make them more interesting.

- Add a teaspoon of mustard and a dash of milk to make mustard mash. Nice with sausages or corned beef fritters.
- Make colcannon: boil potatoes up with thinly sliced bacon and shredded savoy cabbage plus a bit of thyme. Mash with a dash of milk.
- Roast them with rosemary and garlic: scrub and parboil floury potatoes. As you drain them, bash them against the side of the colander to make the outsides fluffy. Meanwhile, heat a little fat in a roasting tin, then toss the parboiled potatoes into it with fresh or dried rosemary and a couple of crushed cloves of garlic if you have it. Both the parboiling and the melting fat first will cut down on how much fat you need to use. Roast for 35–45 minutes until they are golden and crispy on the edges.

- Make rosti with leftover potatoes: when they're cold, grate them coarsely into a bowl. In a heavy frying pan, cook a finely sliced onion in a little fat until soft, then stir it into the potato and season. Return to the pan and pat into a cake. Cook until the underside is golden brown, shaking it frequently to stop any sticking. Place the pan under a heated grill or flip the cake in the pan to cook through the top side. Cut into wedges to serve. These go with anything, including themselves, for breakfast – but they are especially good with fish.

◇◇◇

Stuffed jackets

We love this supper in our house! Bake the potato whole in its jacket. When baked, cut a slit and scoop out the flesh, leaving the skin intact. Mix the flesh with cooked sausage meat, a little grated cheese and onion, or even some cooked flaked fish with parsley and a bit of milk if you like, plus seasoning. It's lovely with a bit of chopped fresh chilli, should you have some on your windowsill. Pile the mixture back into the skin and bring up to heat in the oven.

Leftovers for dinner

"Food is a munition of war! Don't waste it!"

**Lord Woolton,
Minister for Food**

Of course, not wasting food isn't about winning a war now, unless you count the war on want and waste. But it does give you a slight sense of being a kitchen superhero when your bin is empty and your tummy is full. I grew up on leftovers and, although I'd become sloppy about it, this part of the challenge was like putting on a favourite old jumper: as soon as I slipped back into it, it felt comfortable and right. If you're not too sure how to proceed, here are some tips from the Ministry of Food... and also, my mum.

- If you're using up already-cooked food, don't overcook it. Add it last and remember it only needs to be heated through.
- Try and include something fresh with your leftovers, such as green salad. The vitamins break down in reheated food.
- Turn stale bread into breadcrumbs for stuffing and toppings, croutons for soup; or bread puddings or summer puddings, filled with stewed fruit.

Quick risotto

My mum's best standby for weekday meals. Also works with pasta, depending on what you spend your points on. Either use leftover rice or cook up some fresh (you don't need proper risotto rice, ordinary will do). Dice any leftover meat, fish, bacon or vegetables (you can use anything in this, that's the beauty of it). Chop an onion and a bit of garlic and either dry-fry or use a little oil or a touch of stock. Add the cooked leftovers – with a bit more stock if it's getting sticky – and some herbs. Add the rice and stir everything together until it's all heated through and cooked. Add a little more stock as needed. Season and serve.

◇◇◇

Bubble and squeak

So great on a Monday evening after a Sunday roast!

1 chopped onion
4 rashers of bacon, snipped into bits (optional)
About 450 g (1 lb) of mashed potato
Mixed leftover vegetables: parsnips, leeks, cabbage, peas, broccoli – anything you have
25 g (1 oz) cheese
Dash of milk
25 g (1 oz) butter

Method

Fry the onion until soft, then add the bacon bits, if using. Remove from the heat and transfer to a big bowl. Save the pan. Add the mash and vegetables to the bowl, then mix it all up with a dash of milk if it seems a bit dry. Melt a little bit of butter into the pan and add the mash mixture, patting it into a cake. Cook over a medium heat until the underside is browned and the cake is heated through. Sprinkle over some cheese and finish under the grill.

Meat rationing

"For most people the main problem of the meat ration is how to produce substantial tasty dishes throughout the week with the limited amount of meat available daily."

**Ministry of Food leaflet:
"Making the Most of Meat"**

If you're a die-hard carnivore, you're probably going to find the meat ration a little tricky to eke out. The meat ration consisted of 100 g (4 oz) of bacon or ham, and meat to the value of 1s 2d, which I worked out on average to be about 500 g (1 lb 2 oz) meat per week – and I'm afraid we're not talking sirloin steak here. Unlike other parts of the rations allowance, what you'd get in your basket was based on monetary value rather than weight, so if you were willing to eat cheaper cuts you could get more. However, it's still not that massive, so hopefully the following tips will help make it go further. Offal and game were not rationed, but when they were available, it would have been shared out, so not unlimited.

- You're probably tired of hearing this, but the best way to bulk out your meat is to add vegetables. Buying mince or stewing steak is the easiest way to make this happen; add plenty of seasonal and root vegetables and you can make a really good casserole or pie without splurging it all at once.
- Use beans and lentils (available on your points) to add protein.

- Add breadcrumbs, onions, herbs and spices to mince to make homemade burgers.
- Use your points to add corned beef, tinned fish, hot dog sausages or Spam to your monthly meat allowance. (The fat that American hot dogs came in was also a really useful boost to the fat ration.)
- Keep an eye out for seasonal game and offal, which you wouldn't need to spend your rations on.

Basic beef casserole

This is the kind of recipe you can mess about. Change the vegetables, improvise, turn it into a cottage pie... It's a base recipe. Feel free to get creative.

250 g (9 oz) stewing beef or brisket in large chunks

2 leeks, sliced in chunks

1 onion, diced

2 big carrots, sliced thickly

A bay leaf, some thyme and other herbs

About 150-200 ml (8 fl oz) stock

25 g (1 oz) butter or margarine

1 tbsp flour or cornflour

Method

Heat the oven to about 160°C. Brown the beef with the onions in a casserole dish with the butter, then add in the leeks, onion, carrots, and bay leaf. When soft, stir in the flour until it's evenly mixed in with no lumps. Add the stock and any other herbs you fancy and allow to simmer. Pop the lid on and place it all in the oven for at least 1.5 hours until the beef is really tender and the sauce is nice and thick. Serve with some lovely mashed potatoes, bread, rice... you name it.

Jam: Tips and tricks

This is an excellent way to preserve all those fruits you think will never run out in the summer, but will miss dreadfully in the winter if you're living on rations. You will need to save, beg, or borrow sugar rations to get the job done, or just make smaller batches.

Jam tips:

- Use fresh, firm fruit. Overripe fruit can make you poorly.
- Use a big pan – if you fill it too full it will bubble over.
- Stew the fruit first, with just enough water to stop it burning, before adding sugar.
- For 600 g (1 lb 4 oz) of fruit you need approximately 600–800 g (1 lb 4 oz–1 lb 12 oz) of sugar. It sounds a lot, but sugar is the preservative that keeps the jam fresh.
- Boil your jam quickly. Start testing the setting point reasonably early on so you don't break down the pectin too much.
- With fruit that doesn't have much pectin, add citric acid to help it set.
- The setting point of jam is 106°C. These days, you can use a sugar thermometer. In the absence of one, use the wrinkle test: when you think your jam is ready, spoon a little onto a cold plate. Let it stand, then give it a nudge. If the surface wrinkles, then it's ready. If not, put the pan back on the heat and try again on a cold plate in a few minutes.
- Jars should be thoroughly sterilized. Heat the oven to 120°C (fan). Wash the jars in hot, soapy water, then rinse well. Place them on a baking tray and put them in the oven to dry completely. Remove rubber seals if you're using Kilner jars and boil them – dry heat damages them. If you're using pre-used jars and lids, add a wax disc to the top of your jam while it's hot to seal it in.

Wartime raspberry jam

2.75 kg (6 lb) raspberries
2.75 kg (6 lb) sugar

Method

Cook the raspberries slowly until some juice has come out of the fruit. Add the sugar and stir until dissolved. Boil rapidly until the setting point is reached.

◇◇

Wartime green tomato jam

2.75 kg (6 lb) green tomatoes
2.75 kg (6 lb) sugar
75 g (3 oz) root ginger, or ground ginger, to taste
12 allspice berries

Method

Steam the tomatoes until tender, then skin and place in a preserving pan with the sugar and the spices tied in a bit of muslin (or if you're using ground ginger, add it during the boiling by the spoonful). Boil rapidly until the setting point is reached, tasting every now and then to check the flavour.

Wartime pastry and bread

Good pastry was pretty hard to come by in the war years; fat was scarce and flour was wholewheat and thus quite heavy. To compensate for the heaviness, add a bit of extra baking powder to plain flour or use self-raising flour. You can fill wheatmeal or potato pastry with cooked filling and make pasties, or use as a pie crust.

Shortcrust pastry

225 g (8 oz) plain or self-raising flour
Pinch of salt
100 g (4 oz) margarine and lard mixed, or cooking fat
Cold water to bind

Method

Sift the flour and salt and rub in the fat until you have breadcrumbs. Add enough water to make a firm, rollable dough. Use as per your recipe.

◇◇

Wheatmeal pastry

225 g (8 oz) wheatmeal flour
½ tsp salt
1 tsp baking powder
50 g (2 oz) margarine, cooking fat, or dripping

Method

Rub the fat into the combined dry ingredients. Add enough water to make a soft, rollable dough. Use as per your recipe.

Potato pastry

100 g (4 oz) flour
½ tsp salt
25 g (1 oz) cooking fat or lard
225 g (8 oz) mashed potato

Method

Mix the flour with the salt. Rub in the fat with your fingertips, then work into the potato. Mix to a very dry dough with a small quantity of cold water. Knead and roll out.

◇◇

Gran's delicious soda bread

250 g (9 oz) wholemeal flour
250 g (9 oz) plain flour (or use all wholemeal) plus extra for
  dusting
1 tsp bicarbonate of soda
1 tsp salt
450–500 ml (16 fl oz) "household" (reconstituted powdered milk) or
  ordinary milk, and one capful of vinegar

Method

Sift the dry ingredients together in a bowl. Add the milk a bit at a time, and mix until you form a soft dough. Make sure you have a little extra flour to hand as it's sticky to begin with. Tip the dough onto a floured surface and form into a smooth ball. Try not to knead it too much – just gather it up and try to keep the air in. Cut a big deep cross right across the top of your ball with a serrated knife, almost severing it into four. Leave it to sit for 30 minutes. Bake on a floured baking tray at 200°C for about 30 minutes, until it's risen and the slits have closed up again. It should have a nice crust on the outside.

Sweet treats

> "Puddings and sweets are a
> delightful addition to a main meal
> but should only be regarded as such.
> Children particularly should be
> encouraged to eat their first course...
> before they are allowed the
> sweet course."
>
> **War Cookery Leaflet Number 13**

If you have a sweet tooth, I'd recommend investing in some dried fruit with your points and making tea loaves (or barmbrack) – they are fatless and you can make them with less sugar and they'll still taste good.

Dairy-free and low-sugar baking has come a long way since the war, and there are delicious recipes out there. Building on the humble carrot cake, try courgette, squash, beetroot – you name it – to compensate for the lack of fat and sugar. Again, a bit of dried fruit goes a long way!

Save some bread for bread puddings. It cuts waste and really, they taste better than wartime cake.

Steamed puddings were all the rage in the war years and with a bit of custard they're quite presentable.

Basic steamed pudding[47]

225 g (8 oz) flour
50 g (2 oz) sugar
50 g (2 oz) fat
1 dried egg
1 tsp baking powder
Pinch of salt
Water or milk to mix

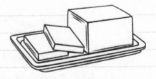

Method

Beat the fat and sugar until light and fluffy. Add the flour
and baking powder in three batches, alternating with the salt
and reconstituted egg. Add enough milk (or water) to make a
dropping consistency. (This means a consistency that drops off
the spoon in a nice dollop when you tip the spoon.) Add fruit or
flavouring, place in a greased pudding basin, cover with greased
baking parchment and steam for 1.5–2 hours. Possible fillings/
flavour suggestions: 2 tbsp treacle, 1 tsp ground ginger, 2 tbsp
golden syrup, 2 tbsp jam or marmalade, 50 g (2 oz) dried fruit.

◇◇

Barmbrack

This is divine with a scrape of butter. (I like mine with cheese but
that could be seen as weird.)

350 g (12 oz) dried fruit
110 g (4 oz) sugar
About 250 ml (8 fl oz) cold black tea
1 egg (fresh or reconstituted)
225 g (8 oz) self-raising flour

Method

Combine the fruit and sugar with the tea in a tub and leave to soak overnight. The next day, add the egg and flour to the mixture. Stir well until combined. Line a loaf tin with greaseproof paper and bake at 180°C for about one hour and 10 minutes or until cooked through. A knife should come out clean when you poke it through the middle.

◇◇

Bread and butter pudding

About 6–8 slices of bread, thinly scraped with butter or margarine

75 g (3 oz) fruit (dried or fresh, chopped)

455 ml (1 pint) custard (find a wartime custard recipe in the "Gather: Spring" section below)

Method

Cube the buttered bread and arrange in a medium pie dish, alternating with the fruit to build layers. Pour the custard over the top. Bake at around 170°C until lightly browned on the top.

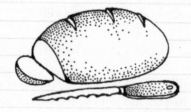

Gather

Bring friends and family together with these delicious, seasonal recipes, which are fine to use when you're on rations and exciting enough to use when you're not. As ever, feel free to improvise, substitute and play according to your rations and your store cupboard.

Spring

MENU 1
Spring Picnic

- Salad in jars
- Asparagus wrapped in bacon
- Wraps with spicy vegetable filling
- Rhubarb and custard slices

Who cares if it's still cold? At the first sign of less soggy days, grab the blankets and baskets and head to the nearest green spot for a picnic. Worth it even if you're still wearing your coat and scarf – just remember to take some nice hot tea in a flask!

Salad in jars

These layered salad jars are so tasty and look
lovely. A packed lunch in a pot. You will need:

A selection of seasonal vegetable and salad items: mixed leaves,
blanched asparagus, red cabbage, carrots, spring onions,
sprouts and seedlings, watercress, beetroot, radishes –
whatever you fancy.

Some vinaigrette or dressing of your choice (I mix one part oil
to two parts vinegar with a little mustard).

A small, clean wide-necked jam jar for each person.

Method

Shred, grate, or finely slice all of the vegetables in separate piles.
One variety at a time, place the vegetables into a bowl and toss
in a little of the vinaigrette. Use a slotted spoon so you leave oil
in the bowl, to share equally between the jars and press down.
Repeat the process for each vegetable item, using the same bowl
to toss the salad so you don't lose the dressing. Pack it down tight
so you can really fill them up. Try and vary the order to create
layers of colour and texture.

◇◇◇

Asparagus wrapped in bacon

Very simply: wash sixteen fresh asparagus spears and blanch in
boiling water. Wrap them in four thinly sliced and halved-longways
streaky bacon rashers and griddle for minute or two on each side
until the bacon is cooked.

◇◇◇

Wraps with spicy vegetable filling

For the wraps:
440 g (1 lb) flour
1 tsp salt
¼ tsp baking powder
250 ml (8 fl oz) warm water

For the filling:
1 finely chopped onion
1 deseeded chopped chilli (or some chilli powder)
1-2 large courgettes
About half a cooked cauliflower, cut up small
6-8 finely diced tomatoes
Fresh coriander
A bunch of sliced spring onions
A sprinkle of cheese or spoonful of cottage cheese per wrap

Method

In a large bowl, stir together the flour, salt and baking powder.
Pour in water; stir to combine. If you need to, add extra water
1 tbsp at a time, until you have a soft, workable dough. Knead
briefly on a lightly floured surface. Divide into sixteen equal
pieces. Cover and leave to rest for 20 minutes. Roll out each
ball on a floured surface with a floured rolling pin until it's thin
and about the same diameter as your frying pan. Heat your
pan, ungreased, over a medium-high heat. Cook the rounds
until brown flecks appear underneath. Flip and cook the other
side. Fry the onion and courgette with the chilli. Add the diced
tomatoes and the cauliflower and cook on a medium heat until
the mixture goes quite thick, and the cauliflower is cooked
through. If the mixture gets too sticky too quickly add a dash
of water. Just before you take the mixture off the heat, add in a
good handful of fresh coriander and stir. Leave to cool. (You can
make this bit up the day before.) When your wraps are made and

it's time to picnic, spoon a heaped dessert spoon of the filling into the centre of the wrap. Add a dollop of cottage cheese or a sprinkle of cheddar, and scatter some chopped spring onions. Roll each wrap up tightly and stack in a plastic lunch box to keep them rolled up. Make these up as near to the time you're taking your picnic out as possible; store in the fridge if you need to make ahead.

Rhubarb and custard slices

Make this ahead of time. To avoid cheating, this uses a wartime custard recipe. You can substitute nicer versions if your wartime work is done.

   1 quantity of shortcrust pastry (see "Wartime pastry
      and bread" earlier in this section).
   5–6 stalks of rhubarb (about 700 g or 1 lb 8 oz)
   4 tbsp sugar
   A cap of vanilla extract or a vanilla pod scraped out
      (if you have it)

Custard:[48]
   2 level tbsp of dried egg
   2 tbsp flour (or cornflour if you have it)
   1 tbsp sugar
   1 tsp cinnamon or nutmeg to taste
   455 ml (1 pint) milk (or household milk)

Method

Roll out your shortcrust pastry into a loose bottomed flan tin, about 25 cm in diameter. Cover with greaseproof paper and fill with baking beans. Bake for 15 minutes at about 170°C, then remove the beans and bake for a further 5 minutes. At the same time, wash the rhubarb, slice into 2 cm sticks and place in a roasting tin. Toss thoroughly in the sugar and vanilla (if using), and roast for about 15–20 minutes at 170°C until it's still in

shape but softened and hot. Take the pastry and rhubarb out
of the oven and leave aside. Sieve the egg, spice and flour into
a heatproof bowl or jug. Add the sugar and mix with a fork.
Pour in a little of the milk to make a smooth paste, then boil
up the rest of the milk and gradually add, whisking constantly
to avoid lumps. If you have it, add a dash more vanilla. Arrange
the rhubarb on top of the pastry and pour the custard on top.
Sprinkle over a little more nutmeg or cinnamon. Bake at 150°C
until the custard is just set (about 30 minutes). When the tart is
cool, pop into the fridge. Before your picnic, take it out and slice
it into eight pieces for your picnic.

Summer

MENU 2
Summer BBQ

- Minced pork kebabs
- Pitta breads
- Barbecued artichokes
  with vinaigrette
- Mini jackets
- Summer pudding with
  mock cream

Quick! The sun's out! Not a moment to lose: round up the troops and get the barbecue going!

Much of this menu can be prepared in advance so it's good to read through before the day. As always, feel free to experiment and substitute. All of these dishes can be done in the oven or under the grill if it's a proper British summer day and thus raining.

NB: Bunting is never over the top.

Minced pork kebabs

650 g (1 lb 4 oz) pork mince
30 g (1 oz) finely ground oatmeal
1 bunch spring onions, finely chopped
1 clove of garlic, crushed
1 small chilli, deseeded and chopped very finely
1 tsp cumin, if you have it (or other spice to taste)
1 pepper, sliced into large chunks
1 courgette, sliced into large chunks
Seasoning

Method

Mix up the pork, oatmeal, spring onion, garlic, chilli, and spices, with salt and pepper to taste. Form into small meatballs, each about the size of a golf ball, then thread the meat onto the skewers, alternating with slices of peppers and courgette. Place the kebabs on the barbecue (at medium heat). Cook, turning once, until browned on both sides and no longer pink in the centre, about 8 minutes.

◇◇◇

Pitta breads

240 ml (8 fl oz) warm (not hot) water
2 tsp fast action dry yeast
500–600 g (1 lb 2 oz–1 lb 4 oz) plain (or wholemeal) flour
2 tsp salt
A little oil (about 2 tbsp)

Method

Sift the flour into a large bowl. Tip in the yeast and salt, on opposite sides of the bowl. Make a well and pour in the water, then mix to form a rough dough. If you have a little oil to spare, oil a clean worktop; otherwise lightly flour it, but try not to add too much extra flour. Turn out the dough and knead until it is smooth and elastic, about 5–10 minutes. Form it into a nice smooth ball. Clean out your bowl and rub a little oil over it. Turn your ball of dough about in the bowl to coat it and then cover with a clean tea towel or cling film until it's doubled: at least an hour. After that you can refrigerate the dough until you need it; it will keep for up to a week. Preheat the oven to 220°C and heat up two baking trays. Divide up your dough into eight pieces and roll into balls, then roll them out into flat circles about half a centimetre thick. Place them on the hot trays and bake for 5–10 minutes until they magically puff up and just start to brown. Wrap the pittas in a clean tea towel to cool. So lovely if baked and eaten on the same day, but you can freeze or refrigerate them.

◇◇

Barbecued artichokes with vinaigrette

2 artichokes
Oil, vinegar, mustard

Method

Easy peasy: steam the artichokes until tender but not overly soft – they should still hold together. Brush with a small amount of oil, season and pop them on a medium barbecue until they begin to char slightly. This is real friendship food; when they feel slightly cool to the touch, you can tug the leaves off and dip them in vinaigrette (use one part oil to two parts vinegar with a scant teaspoon of mustard).

◇◇◇◇◇◇◇◇◇◇◇◇◇◇◇◇◇◇◇◇◇◇◇◇◇◇◇◇◇◇◇◇◇◇◇◇◇◇◇

Mini jackets

500 g (1 lb 2 oz) new potatoes
A little coarse sea salt
Finely grated cheddar or cottage cheese
Fresh chopped chives

Method

Wash the potatoes and prick with a fork. Toss with sea salt. Wrap each mini spud in foil and place on the barbecue. They should bake in about 30–40 minutes. Alternatively, you can bake them on a tray in the oven (unfoiled) at 180°C for about the same time. Let the potatoes cool for a bit, then cut a small cross in the top of each and pinch the bases to open them out. Fill each with a teaspoon of cottage cheese or cheddar, sprinkle with chives and serve. Hint: if you had a bit of bacon you could finely dice it, fry it up and add it in with the cheddar. So yum!

◇◇◇◇◇◇◇◇◇◇◇◇◇◇◇◇◇◇◇◇◇◇◇◇◇◇◇◇◇◇◇◇◇◇◇◇◇◇◇

Summer pudding

About 7 slices of day-old bread (crusts removed)

170 g (6 oz) sugar

1 kg (2 lb 4 oz) of mixed summer berries (try blackberries, bilberries, redcurrants, cherries, raspberries... there are so many to choose from! Strawberries aren't so great for this recipe, however. If you want to use them, keep them separate and add them in to the fruit mix just before you put it in the pudding basin).

Method

Wash fruit and gently dry on kitchen paper. Put the sugar and 3 tbsp water into a large pan. Heat until the sugar dissolves, stirring, then add in the berries. Cook for a few minutes over a low heat, stirring occasionally until the fruit softens but is still intact. Sieve the fruit over a bowl or jug to catch the juice. Line a deep 1 litre (1.75 pint) pudding basin with cling film (this helps the pudding come out at the end) and let it hang over the sides by about 15 cm. Keep one piece of bread whole and cut two into quarter triangles. Cut the rest in half lengthways, slightly on the diagonal to make uneven rectangles.

Dip the whole piece of bread into the berry juice and press it into the bottom of the bowl. Then dip the uneven rectangles in juice one at a time and press around the basin's sides so that they fit together neatly, alternately placing wide and narrow ends up. You may need to trim the last bit to fit it in. Now spoon in the softened fruit. Dip the quarter triangles in juice and arrange on the top. Bring the cling film up and loosely seal. Put a side plate on the top and chill the pudding overnight. Save any leftover juice in the fridge as well. To serve, open out the cling film then put a serving plate upside down on top and flip over. Serve with leftover juice, any extra berries and mock cream if you like.

Mock cream

1 tbsp cornflour
25 g (1 oz) margarine or butter
25 g (1 oz) sugar (preferably caster or icing, or
   blitz granulated in the blender if you can!)
150 ml (0.25 pint) milk

Method

Blend the cornflour and 1 tbsp milk together until a thick and smooth paste forms. Put the rest of the milk in a saucepan, add the paste and stir over a low heat until thickened. Remove and cool completely. Cream butter or margarine and sugar together until light and fluffy, then gradually add in the cold cornflour/milk mixture a bit at a time until all of it is mixed together to make a smooth, thick cream. This will stiffen up in the fridge and is best served cold when you're ready for it.

Autumn

MENU 3
Autumn
Supper

- Stuffed mini squashes

- Game casserole with celeriac and potato mash with wilted greens

- Blackberry bread and butter pudding

Autumn is the season of abundance. Delicious nutty flavours begin creeping in, and as the weather gets colder, more substantial root vegetables form the basis of comforting stews and casseroles. Perfect for cosy suppers with friends after a long walk through the autumn leaves... Why not forage for chestnuts while you're out and about! **NB: NEVER forage mushrooms without expert guidance.**

Stuffed mini squashes

  8 mini acorn squashes
  455 ml (1 pint) cooked rice
  2 onions, finely diced
  2 cloves of garlic, smashed and chopped

A couple of handfuls of chestnuts, roasted, shelled and mashed
up a bit
A couple of handfuls of wild mushrooms, chopped small
Sage (preferably fresh leaves but dried will do)
Enough strong blue cheese to sprinkle a bit over each squash –
or, if you're being strict, use cheddar

Method

Slice the tops off the squashes. Scoop out all the seeds and
discard. Rub a little oil onto the flesh of each squash and season.
Preheat the oven to 180°C. Make the stuffing: fry the onions
until softened then add the garlic. Cook for another minute,
then add the mushrooms, chestnuts and torn sage leaves. Cook
on a medium heat, adding a little bit of water or stock if it
begins to stick. When everything's nicely cooked through, add
in the rice and mix it all up. Then fill your squashes with the rice
stuffing and crumble a little cheese over the top. Return to the
oven for a further 15–20 minutes, until the squash is tender, the
cheese is melted and the filling is cooked through. The skin of
the squash should still be quite rigid, but the flesh will break up
into delicious ribbons.

◇◇◇

Game casserole

Game wasn't rationed which is an advantage, although there
wouldn't have been an unlimited supply, and it may be more tricky
to come by these days. Check the seasonal calendar and ask your
local supplier for what's available. You can also substitute beef but
bear in mind this would be rationed.

About 1 kg (2 lb 4 oz) diced mixed game
Flour to coat the game
3-4 rashers streaky bacon, diced

8–9 shallots, halved lengthways
1 stick of celery, chopped
500 g (1 lb 2 oz) carrots (mixed colours if you can get them),
    scrubbed and sliced
2 cloves of garlic, crushed and chopped
300 g (10.5 oz) wild mushrooms
600 ml (1 pint) stock (preferably beef)
Bay leaves, rosemary, sage

Method

Heat your oven to 150°C. Toss the game in the flour, then fry it in batches in a large casserole with a couple of tablespoons of oil. When it's browned, lift it from the pan and set aside. In the same pan, add another tablespoon of oil and fry the bacon, then the shallots. Add the celery, carrots and garlic and stir over a low heat until they soften. Add the meat back in, along with the herbs and mushrooms. Stir everything, then add the stock and season. Bring to a simmer. Put the lid on and cook for 2.5–3 hours until the meat is tender.

◇◇

Celeriac and potato mash with wilted greens

2 celeriac
4 large-ish potatoes
A little butter
A dash of milk, or sour cream if you have it
Spinach, spring greens or other leafy green vegetables

Method

Peel and roughly chop the celeriac and potatoes. Boil them together in a pan of salted water for about 20 minutes or until soft. Mash them with the butter and milk or sour cream. Wash

the spinach, spring greens or other leafy green vegetables. Set
them in a steamer or a sieve over a pan of simmering water and
cover with a lid for about 7 minutes until they are nice and
soft. Share out the celeriac mash between warm plates. Add the
drained greens to the top and spoon on the hot casserole.

◇◇

Blackberry Bread and Butter Pudding

8 slices of bread, buttered
900 ml (1.5 pints) of custard (wartime recipe
    in the "Gather: Spring" section above)
300–450 g (11–14 oz) blackberries
2 tbsp sugar (brown if you have it), golden syrup or treacle
Grated nutmeg (optional)

Method

Set the blackberries to simmer with the sugar/syrup and enough
water to stop them sticking to the pan. Cook until they are
softened but still holding their shape. Arrange four of the slices
of bread in the bottom of a medium baking dish, then pour
over the blackberry compote. Press the next four slices over the
top. Pour the custard over the top, sprinkle over a little grated
nutmeg, and bake at around 170°C until the top is browned.

Winter

MENU 4
Christmas Feast

- Yuletide pierogi

- Veggie Christmas pie

- Roasted root vegetables

- Christmas fruity cupcakes
  topped with wartime mock
  marzipan

I love the winter months. For me, it's about cosying in, candlelight, silly jokes and gathering friends. This Christmas buffet makes the most of Yuletide flavours while trying not to cut too much into your rations. Amazing what you can do with free food!

There's a lovely Winter Wonder soup recipe in the "Soups" section if you fancy adding a soup course.

Yuletide *Pierogi* [49]

Pierogi are Polish dumplings and they are delicious. These have been adapted to incorporate some Christmassy fillings.

For the dough:

125 g (4 oz) self-raising flour
Pinch of salt
½ tsp vegetable oil
75 ml (2.5 fl oz) warm water

Flour

For the first filling:
  2 rashers of bacon (finely diced)
  2 mashed up sausages (or the equivalent in sausage meat)
  1 good dessert spoon of cranberries
For the second filling:
  1 small diced onion
  75 g (3 oz) finely chopped mushrooms
  75 g (3 oz) cooked, diced chestnuts

Method

Sift the flour into a large mixing bowl and make a well in the centre. Fill the well with the salt, oil and water. Stir the flour into the wet ingredients and bring together as a soft dough. Turn onto a lightly floured work surface and knead for 5–8 minutes, or until it's smooth and glossy. Wrap the dough ball in a clean tea towel and set aside to rest in a cool room for at least 20 minutes. Meanwhile make the fillings. Fry the bacon and sausages/sausage meat. Add the cranberries. Stir until well cooked and mixed. Separately, fry the onion with the mushrooms. Tip into a separate bowl and add the chestnuts. Chop and mix together. When the dough has rested, roll it out on a lightly floured surface. It should be about 3 mm thick. Use a 10 cm round biscuit cutter to make circles of dough. Divide the circles into two batches, add 1 tsp of the sausage and bacon cranberry filling to one batch and 1 tsp of the mushroom and chestnut filling to the other. Brush the edge of each pastry round with water and fold them over to make little pasty shapes, pinching the edges together to seal. Poach the *pierogi*, in batches if necessary, in a deep pan of boiling water for 3–4 minutes, or until they float to the surface. Pile them onto serving plates. These are wonderful with a little sour cream drizzled over if you can get it, but if you're eating in wartime, fear not, they taste lovely without.

Veggie Christmas pie[50]

You can alter the fillings according to your taste and what you have; you can also use one quantity of pastry and just make a pie top instead of a full pie. You can also make this pie the day before, and store it wrapped in cling film in the fridge until you're ready to bake it.

2 quantities of shortcrust pastry (recipe in "Wartime pastry and bread" earlier in this section)
25 g (1 oz) butter
300 g (10.5 oz) leeks, thinly sliced
200 g (7 oz) Brussels sprouts, shredded
1 punnet mushrooms (about 250 g or 9 oz), any variety, chopped
200 g (7 oz) parsnip, grated
200 g (7 oz) cooked lentils
100 g (4 oz) cooked chestnuts, chopped
100 g (4 oz) cranberries
dried thyme or other herbs to taste
200 ml (6 fl oz) milk
1 tbsp cornflour mixed with 1 tbsp water

Method

Fry the leeks and Brussels sprouts in about half the butter. Add in the mushrooms and cook until they're softened, then drain any excess liquid and add the herbs. Add in the grated parsnip and cook for a couple more minutes, then add the lentils and chestnuts. Keep stirring over a medium heat and let the flavours blend. Add the cranberries and remove from the heat.

Heat the milk and tip in the cornflour paste. Stir over a medium heat until the milk thickens. Pour enough milk over the veggie mix to make sure everything is nicely moistened, but don't drown it or you'll get soggy pastry.

Grease a large-ish, deep-sided pie dish with a little of the butter. Roll out one quantity of pastry on a floured surface and use it to line the dish. Let the pastry edges overhang a little bit. Spoon in the veggie mixture and pat evenly into place. Roll out the second quantity of pastry. Use a small Christmas cookie cutter to cut a couple of festive holes in the top (save these) and place the pie lid over the pie. Crimp the edges to seal with the bottom pastry and scatter the saved Christmas shapes on the top. At this point you can refrigerate the pie.

When you're ready to bake, heat the oven to 220°C. Brush the pastry top with a little milk and bake for about half an hour, or longer if necessary, until the pie crust is golden and the filling is steaming out of the holes.

Serve with extra cranberry sauce or gravy as you like, and some roasted root vegetables.

Roasted root vegetables

A generous bunch of carrots (preferably multi-coloured if you can find them), scrubbed and halved lengthways

  1 swede
  4 parsnips
  1 raw beetroot
  1 celeriac

Method

Peel the vegetables and cut them into chunks. Toss them lightly in oil, melted fat, or dripping. Add some thyme, rosemary, or other herbs and season. Roast at 220°C for about 40–50 minutes.

Christmas fruity cupcakes

Really this recipe is worthy of your fresh eggs but, if you don't have them, use reconstituted.

140 g (5.5 oz) dried fruit (any you can get but if you can get
   a mix with some candied peel, cherries, cranberries and so
   on, hurrah!)
3 tbsp tea (or substitute rum if you have it)
2 eggs
60 g (2 oz) sugar (preferably brown, but what you have)
140 g (5 oz) carrot, very finely grated
60 g (2 oz) plain flour
35 g (1.25 oz) ground hazelnuts
1.5 tsp baking powder
1 tsp each of ginger, nutmeg and mixed spice
Pinch of salt

Method

Soak the fruit in the tea (or rum). Meanwhile whisk the eggs and sugar with the salt until they're fluffy. Stir in the carrot. Add the flour, hazelnuts, soaked fruit, spice and baking powder and fold until the dry ingredients are thoroughly incorporated, but don't overmix. Fill up nine deep cupcake cases in a muffin tin and bake for about half an hour at 180°C. When these are cool, you can serve them as they are, ice them with a little water icing and a few silvery cake sprinkles if you have them, top with a little mock marzipan (recipe below) or even serve with a little mock cream on the side (see recipe in the "Gather: Summer" section).

Wartime mock marzipan

The original recipe calls for soya flour but you can use plain flour instead. Soya flour was available during the war and often promoted as an alternative.

144

1 tbsp water
25 g (1 oz) margarine
1 tsp almond essence
50 g (2 oz) sugar or syrup
50 g (2 oz) soya flour (or plain flour)

Method

Melt the margarine in water, add the almond essence and sugar, then the flour. Turn onto a surface and knead well. It can be a little flakier than normal marzipan but you should be able to beat it sufficiently into submission to flatten it out and cut some Christmas stars with a shaped cutter for the tops of your cupcakes.

Seasonal
Calendar

Seasonal food wasn't rationed during the Second World War, as only those foods which could be guaranteed all year round were added to the rations list. But, of course, the fruit, vegetables and other food which became available month by month was a vital addition to the rationed plate.

Nowadays, many of us are returning to seasonal eating, which cuts food waste and carbon emissions, supports local producers, and means getting everything at its nutritional best. It's also a wonderful way to connect with nature and the bounty of every season.

When you're living on rations, having a better knowledge of what's available in each season can really help with the monotony of rations. Even in dismal January, there's far, far more on offer than you might think!

While doing the rations challenge, do check the country of origin on the foods you buy. If it's not from the UK, bear in mind it wouldn't have been available to the wartime kitchen!

NB: Although fish was plentiful off the coast of Britain, getting hold of it in wartime was not always an easy task. What with all the potential U-boats and sea mines off the coast, most fishermen were reluctant to risk it. Fish wasn't rationed, but that was largely because the supply couldn't be guaranteed, not because it was always plentiful.

Spring

Vegetables	artichoke, asparagus, aubergine, beetroot, broccoli, cabbage, carrot, cauliflower, chicory, cucumber, kale, leek, lettuce and salad leaves, marrow, morel mushrooms, new potatoes, parsnip, peas, peppers, purple sprouting broccoli, radish, rocket, salsify, samphire, sorrel, spinach, spring greens, spring onion, swede, watercress, wild nettles
Fruit	rhubarb
Meat	duck, hare, rabbit, venison, lamb, wood pigeon
Fish	cockles, cod, coley, crab, dab, Dover sole, gurnard, haddock, hake, langoustine, lemon sole, lobster, mussels, oysters, plaice, prawns, red mullet, salmon, sardines, shrimp, sea trout, whelks, whitebait, winkles
Herbs and spices	basil, chervil, chilli, chives, coriander, dill, elderflower, oregano, mint, nasturtium, parsley (curly), rosemary, sage, sorrel, tarragon

Summer

Vegetables	asparagus, artichoke, aubergine, beetroot, broad beans, broccoli, cauliflower, carrot, chicory, courgette, cucumber, fennel, French beans, garlic, kohlrabi, leek, lettuce and salad leaves, mangetout, marrow, new potatoes, onion, pak choi, peas, peppers, potato, radish, rocket, runner beans, samphire, sorrel, spinach, spring greens, spring onions, summer squash, sweetcorn, Swiss chard, tomato, turnip, watercress, wild nettles
Fruit	bilberries, blackberries, blackcurrants, blueberries, cherries, damsons, gooseberries, greengages, raspberries, redcurrants, rhubarb, strawberries, tayberries
Meat	lamb, rabbit, venison, wood pigeon
Fish	cod, coley, crab, Dover sole, grey mullet, haddock, halibut, herring, langoustine, lemon sole, mackerel, monkfish, pilchard, plaice, pollack, prawns, red mullet, salmon, sardines, scallops (queen), sea bass (wild), sea bream, sea trout, shrimp, squid, whelks, whitebait
Herbs and spices	basil, chervil, chilli, chives, coriander, dill, elderflower, fennel, oregano, mint, nasturtium, parsley (curly), parsley (flat-leafed), rosemary, sage, sorrel, tarragon, thyme

Autumn

Vegetables	artichoke, aubergine, beetroot, broccoli, Brussels sprouts, butternut squash, cabbage, carrot, cauliflower, celeriac, celery, chicory, courgette, cucumber, fennel, French beans, garlic, horseradish, Jerusalem artichoke, kale, kohlrabi, leek, lettuce, mangetout, marrow, onion, parsnip, pak choi, peas, peppers, potato, pumpkin, radish, rocket, runner beans, salsify, samphire, shallots, sorrel, spinach, spring greens, spring onions, summer squash, swede, sweetcorn, Swiss chard, tomato, turnip, watercress, wild mushrooms, winter squash
Fruit	apples, bilberries, blackberries, crab apples, cranberries, damsons, elderberries, medlar, pears, plums, quince, raspberries, redcurrants, rhubarb, sloes, strawberries
Meat	beef, duck, goose, grouse, guinea fowl, hare, lamb, partridge, pheasant, rabbit, turkey, venison, wood pigeon
Fish	clams, cod, coley, crab, dab, Dover sole, grey mullet, gurnard, haddock, halibut, hake, herring, lemon sole, lobster, mackerel, monkfish, mussels, oysters, pilchard, plaice, pollack, prawns, red mullet, sea bass (wild), sea bream, shrimp, skate, squid, turbot, whelks, winkles
Herbs and spices	chestnuts, chicory, chilli, chives, cobnuts, coriander, hazelnuts, oregano, mint, parsley (curly), parsley (flat-leafed), rosemary, sage, sorrel, thyme

Winter

Vegetables	beetroot, Brussels sprouts, cabbage, carrot, cauliflower, celeriac, celery, chicory, horseradish, Jerusalem artichoke, kale, kohlrabi, leek, mushrooms, onion, parsnip, potato, pumpkin, purple sprouting broccoli, red cabbage, salsify, shallots, spring greens, spring onions, squash, swede, Swiss chard, turnip, watercress, wild mushrooms, winter squash
Fruit	apples, cranberries, pears
Meat	duck, goose, grouse, guinea fowl, hare, partridge, pheasant, rabbit, turkey, venison, wild boar, woodcock
Fish	clams, cockles, cod, coley, crab, dab, Dover sole, gurnard, haddock, halibut, hake, langoustine, lemon sole, lobster, mackerel, monkfish, mussels, oysters, plaice, red mullet, scallops (queen), sea bass (wild), sea bream, skate, turbot, winkles
Nuts	Chestnuts

Conclusion

Wherever we are in our lives, whatever our circumstances or income, it can never hurt to be more connected to the planet, systems, and societies that sustain us. When I completed my original challenge, I felt my eyes opening to so many issues I had known were there but had never really grappled with in a meaningful way.

But more surprisingly, as I went through those days of potatoes and cabbage and waiting for an egg, something else happened. I started to discover a deep and rich joy, because when you have less materially you instinctively reach out more spiritually. You become more aware of the people in your life, and the places you move through.

Sometimes this begins purely as a distraction. If your tummy is growling a bit, it's good to take your mind off it. If your dinner is a bit boring, what else can you do to liven things up?

But something I have also found is that when you live on less you need to live in community more. Want breeds the need for friendship, mutual support, and creativity. It is no lie that "necessity is the mother of invention".

And never was there a truer fairy tale than "Nail Soup": the old story of a woman who only has water for her soup pot, but ingredients are gradually donated by neighbours and friends until she has a fine meal to share. A bunch of carrots on its own is unappealing, but take it to a friend who has an onion and a bit of coriander and you will both be getting somewhere.

Living on little – especially in the last few years of doing it for real – has opened me up to the most unlikely but wonderful friendships: to finding unexpected gems of wisdom, kindness, and love in my own back yard.

I hope you have enjoyed this book, and that bits of it, at least, have spoken to you, informed you, or made you think. The most wonderful outcome would be if it has inspired you to set it aside for a moment, put on your jacket, and take a walk. Perhaps to knock on a neighbour's door, to smile at someone on the bus, or just to take five minutes to stand still and breathe. Whatever you need to feel more connected to your life and your world, I hope you can find time to do just that, and to hold that feeling as precious.

Because the truth about Blitz spirit is that it was underpinned by the feeling that we are all in this together, and that we can help each other through. That is a beautiful thing. With imagination, kindness, friendship, and a sense of fun, the most meagre provisions can become a feast.

References and Further Reading

1   Defra, *Food Statistics Pocketbook 2016*, https://assets.publishing.
    service.gov.uk/government/uploads/system/uploads/attachment_data/
    file/553390/foodpocketbook-2016report-rev-15sep16.pdf,
    p. 42.

2   Defra, *Food Statistics Pocketbook*, https://assets.publishing.service.
    gov.uk/government/uploads/system/uploads/attachment_data/
    file/553390/foodpocketbook-2016report-rev-15sep16.pdf, p. 45.

3   Steve Goodier, "Use your greatest power": http://www.
    LifeSupportSystem

4   UN News, "UN adopts new global goals", 25 September 2015,
    https://news.un.org/en/story/2015/09/509732-un-adopts-new-
    global-goals-charting-sustainable-development-people-and-planet#.
    WFBNo_mLSUk.

5   British Coffee Association, https://www.britishcoffeeassociation.org/
    coffee-in-the-uk/coffee-facts.

6   Fairtrade, "Breaking Fast: why it's time to wake up to the hunger
    behind our breakfast", https://www.fairtrade.org.uk/~/media/
    fairtradeuk/media%20centre/documents/fairtrade_breaking_fast_
    report.ashx, p. 8.

7   Fairtrade, "Breaking Fast", https://www.fairtrade.org.uk/~/media/
    fairtradeuk/media%20centre/documents/fairtrade_breaking_fast_
    report.ashx.

8 "What Fairtrade does", Fairtrade, http://www.fairtrade.org.uk/What-is-Fairtrade/What-Fairtrade-does.

9 UN News, "UN adopts new global goals", https://news.un.org/en/story/2015/09/509732-un-adopts-new-global-goals-charting-sustainable-development-people-and-planet.

10 Join me in the 1900s, "Everyday Life, early-mid 20th century, by people who were there", https://www.1900s.org.uk/1940s50s-pig-food-collection.htm.

11 British Library, "Learning", http://www.bl.uk/learning/timeline/item107597.html.

12 Michael Leapman, "Allotments: a very British passion", *The Telegraph*, 10 August 2015, https://www.telegraph.co.uk/gardening/4699817/Allotments-a-very-British-passion.html.

13 Ashley Cowburn, "Households wasted 7.3 million tonnes of food in 2015, new figures reveal", *The Independent*, 10 January 2017, https://www.independent.co.uk/news/uk/politics/uk-household-food-waste-7-million-tonnes-government-defra-caroline-lucas-green-party-mp-a7517931.html.

14 British Hen Welfare Trust, "Chickens remain UK's sixth most popular pet", 4 July 2017, https://www.bhwt.org.uk/chickens-remain-uks-sixth-popular-pet.

15 Hazel Southam, "Allotments are a 'way of life' not a plot of land", *The Telegraph*, 11 August 2018, https://www.telegraph.co.uk/news/2018/08/11/allotments-way-life-not-plot-land-says-national-society-battle.

16 UN News, "UN adopts new global goals", https://news.un.org/en/story/2015/09/509732-un-adopts-new-global-goals-charting-sustainable-development-people-and-planet.

17 The Women's Institute, "What is the Jam Connection?" https://www.thewi.org.uk/faqs/what-is-the-jam-connection.

18 Royal Voluntary Service, "Our History", https://www.royalvoluntaryservice.org.uk/about-us/our-history.

19 BBC, "WW2 People's War", http://www.bbc.co.uk/history/ww2peopleswar/timeline/factfiles/nonflash/a6652055.shtml.

20 BBC, "Did WW2 change life for women?", http://www.bbc.co.uk/guides/z2j9d2p.

21 The WI, "About the WI", https://www.thewi.org.uk/about-the-wi.

22 United Nations Statistics Division, "The World's Women 2015", Chapters 3-5, https://unstats.un.org/unsd/gender/worldswomen.html.

23 Women and Children First, https://www.womenandchildrenfirst.org. uk.

24 Ana Revenga and Sudhir Shetty, International Monetary Fund, "Empowering Women in Smart Economics", March 2012, http:// www.imf.org/external/pubs/ft/fandd/2012/03/revenga.htm

25 Graduate Women International, "Health Outcomes", http://www. graduatewomen.org/the-cause/health-outcomes.

26 Katrin Elborgh-Woytek et al., IMF Staff Discussion Note, "Women, Work & the Economy", September 2013, http://www.imf.org/ external/pubs/ft/sdn/2013/sdn1310.pdf.

27 Elborgh-Woytek et al., "Women, Work & the Economy".

28 Marguerite Patten, *The Victory Cookbook*, Octopus, 1995, p. 11.

29 Take a look at https://www.trusselltrust.org to find out what the organization is currently doing about food poverty.

30 Food and Agriculture Organization of the United Nations, "Sustainable Development Goals", http://www.fao.org/3/a-i7556e.pdf.

31 Food and Agricultural Organization of the United Nations, "Key facts on food loss and waste you should know!", http://www.fao.org/save-food/resources/keyfindings/en.

32 Cooks Info, "British Wartime Food", https://www.cooksinfo.com/ british-wartime-food.

33 Polly Frost, "Julia Child", *Interview Magazine*, 16 July 2009, https:// www.interviewmagazine.com/culture/julia-child.

34 Fairtrade, "Powering up smallholder farmers to make food fair", May 2013, https://www.fairtrade.net/fileadmin/user_upload/content/2009/ news/2013-05-Fairtrade_Smallholder_Report_FairtradeInternational. pdf.

35 Fairtrade, http://www.fairtrade.org.uk.

36 Sarah Morrison, "Too much power in too few hands", *Independent*, 24 February 2013, https://www.independent.co.uk/life-style/food-and-drink/news/too-much-power-in-too-few-hands-food-giants-take-over-the-industry-8508259.html.

37 World Hunger Education Service, https://www.worldhunger.org/world-hunger-and-poverty-facts-and-statistics.

38 Angelique Chrisafis, "French law forbids food waste by supermarkets", *The Guardian*, 4 February 2016, https://www.theguardian.com/world/2016/feb/04/french-law-forbids-food-waste-by-supermarkets.

39 Rebecca Smithers, "Tesco to scrap 'best before' dates from fruit and vegetable lines", *The Guardian*, 8 October 2018, https://www.theguardian.com/environment/2018/oct/08/tesco-to-scrap-best-before-dates-from-fruit-and-vegetable-lines.

40 Iceland, "Iceland & palm oil – haven't we done well?", https://www.iceland.co.uk/environment.

41 FareShare, "New surplus food fund will create almost 250 million meals for good causes", 1 October 2018, https://fareshare.org.uk/new-surplus-food-fund-will-create-almost-250-million-meals-for-good-causes.

42 British Hen Welfare Trust, "Up with the chickens", https://www.bhwt.org.uk/up-with-the-chickens.

43 Peace Pledge Union, "White poppy sales break all records", 8 November 2018, https://ppu.org.uk/news/white-poppy-sales-break-all-records.

44 The Great Get Together, https://www.greatgettogether.org.

45 Claud Fullwood, "Meet thwps://www.thecanary.co/feature/2019/01/13/meet-the-economics-student-turning-landfill-into-food.

46 Ministry of Food Leaflet Number 15.

47 War Cookery Leaflet 13.

48 Taken from Ministry of Food leaflet, "Lashings of Custard".

49 This traditional Polish dish has been adapted with the author's own recipe for the filling.

50 This recipe is adapted from http://www.bbcgoodfood.com/recipes/1799642/individual-christmas-pies. Recipe has been adapted by Lion Hudson for the purposes of this book, adaptations have not been tested by BBC Good Food.

Acknowledgments

This book is a product of a lot of love, teamwork and support and I am hugely grateful. There are countless people to thank but it wouldn't be right not to mention these ones by name:

My husband Ben, who is my soul-mate, my sounding board, and my support, and never fails to make me smile. Thank you for encouraging, listening, suggesting, and helping. Thank you for looking after the kids, and the business, while I worked. I love you so much.

My brilliant children, Violet and Hector, who make every day a feast of fun and never for a second entertain the idea that I might not be able to do something. Thank you. (But I actually can't make pancakes during the school run. It's just not a thing). I love you.

All those strong women: my amazing Mum, who knows more about make-do-and-mend than anyone I ever met and who fed the five thousand on "five loaves and two fishes" every day; Grandma, whom I miss dreadfully; Maddie, Alicia, Helen and Bec, who teach me every day about myself and the world, keep me on my toes and have such wisdom, strength and kindness to share: thank you. I love our tribe and I love you.

To the brilliant editorial team at Lion Hudson – past and present – for your amazing efforts in making this into a book: a huge thank you for all your work, patience and good humour.

In particular, I must thank the wonderful people who were generous enough to contribute and share their enthusiasm and passion with me. That of course includes Elaine, Patricia, Jim, Peggy, Yolande, and Andrew – all of whom shared their stories; and Barney, who shared his culinary brilliance to make a mountain out of a rations molehill. Thank you.

Jim, you have left a larger-than-life gap in the world. You are so missed, and I am so grateful I got to hear your story and write it down before you went.

I am always and forever inspired and humbled by the generation who brought us through the war years and formed the foundations of so much that is good in our country. In particular, Marguerite Patten, the Women's Institute, the Women's Land Army, and everyone who kept Britain going during that long and dark time. Also, Harry Leslie Smith, who lived through those years, the ones before, and the ones after, and was one of the most insightful and righteous voices in today's world. I hope that my generation can truly do yours justice: bringing the messages of hope, peace, acceptance, community, and common sense to all we do. We have so much to learn from you; thank you.

Picture credits

p. 27 Pictorial Press Ltd/Alamy Stock Photo;
pp. 29, 65, 79, 105 (middle), 109, 110 (upper top, upper and lower bottom), 111 (lower), 113, 114, 116, 118, 120 (bottom), 127, 128, 131, 136, 138, 141, 142, 143 Svesla Tasla/Shutterstock;
p. 33 Aquir/istockphoto.com;
pp. 42, 122, 125, 132, 139 (lower) Vectorgoods Studio/Shutterstock;
p. 52 (top) World History Archive/Alamy Stock Photo;
p. 52 (bottom) Stocktrek Images, Inc./Alamy Stock Photo;
p. 57 Geo Images/Alamy Stock Vector;
p. 58 RTRO/Alamy Stock Vector;
p. 74 (bottom) Findlay/Alamy Stock Photo;
p. 102 RetroClipArt/Shutterstock;
pp. 104, 105, 106, 111 (top), 121, 123, 124, 135 Victoria Sergeeva/Shutterstock;
pp. 107 (bottom), 119, 120 (top), 134, 139 (upper) Epine/Shutterstock;
pp. 110 (lower top), 129, 133, 140, 153 Senpo/Shutterstock.

Cover image and chapter opening pages: gud_zyk/istockphoto.com